Social Media Survivor

*The Journey of the President
and CEO of Involver*

Social Media Survivor

Don Beck

SOCIAL MEDIA SURVIVOR
THE JOURNEY OF THE PRESIDENT AND CEO OF INVOLVER

iUniverse books may be ordered through booksellers or by contacting:

iUniverse
1663 Liberty Drive
Bloomington, IN 47403
www.iuniverse.com
1-800-Authors (1-800-288-4677)

Because of the dynamic nature of the Internet, any web addresses or links contained in this book may have changed since publication and may no longer be valid. The views expressed in this work are solely those of the author and do not necessarily reflect the views of the publisher, and the publisher hereby disclaims any responsibility for them.

Any people depicted in stock imagery provided by Thinkstock are models, and such images are being used for illustrative purposes only.
Certain stock imagery © Thinkstock.

ISBN: 978-1-4917-6171-7 (sc)
ISBN: 978-1-4917-6247-9 (hc)
ISBN: 978-1-4917-6174-8 (e)

Library of Congress Control Number: 2015905291

Print information available on the last page.

iUniverse rev. date: 04/28/2015

To my family. My wife, Suzy, has stood by me for many years regardless of the sacrifices associated with my career aspirations. She has always been the foundation of our wonderful family, and I am very fortunate to have her in my life.

My three children, Lindsay, Danny, and Ryan, are the source of my inspiration. I strive every day to make them proud. I could not have accomplished a thing in my career without their support. I am truly a blessed man.

Contents

Introduction

EVER WONDER WHAT IT would be like to be the CEO of a hot, fast-growing social-media start-up in Silicon Valley?

Imagine your feelings of accomplishment and self-satisfaction in becoming one of those famous Internet millionaires from Silicon Valley. You took an idea that you hatched and turned it into a brilliant start-up, which then became the talk of the technology industry. As the CEO, you led the start-up company to a successful exit strategy that made every employee richer than in his or her wildest dreams. You walk the streets of Palo Alto being recognized as an innovator and a visionary in the high-tech industry, elevated with the likes of Steven Jobs of Apple, Sergey Brin and Larry Page of Google, and Mark Zuckerberg of Facebook. The local venture-capitalist community eagerly approaches you to fund your next great idea. You have achieved recognition and financial rewards that most people only dream of in their lives.

These dreams do not come easy or often. The task of taking a good idea and formulating a company that grows into a leader within an industry doesn't come without great sacrifice. The odds are against you. More often, your hard work leads to more start-up failures than company success.

You often read about the start-up that becomes a huge success by leading the initial founders and investors to a profitable exit via an acquisition or initial public offering. (This is when a company initially offers shares of its stock to the general public. An IPO is the first time the owners of the company give up part of that ownership to stockholders.) It sounds so enticing.

But what you rarely hear about are the sacrifices made in order to achieve this success—the ups and downs associated with running a start-up with minimal financial and personnel resources. Every dollar is scrutinized before being spent. Insurmountable challenges are overcome. More often than not, it is a wild ride that has to be experienced to be believed.

I had a chance in my career to experience this excitement firsthand a few years ago. One of the greatest experiences of my thirty-two-year professional career happened when I accepted the role of president and chief executive officer of Involver, a social-media start-up, in September 2011. Although I felt extremely qualified for this responsibility, nothing could prepare me for the highs and lows of leading a small but fast-growing social-media marketing company in a competitive industry that was constantly changing. Every day brought new challenges—not only within the company, but it seemed there were industry announcements that occurred every day that had relevance to Involver and its future. Although our exit was exciting, the events leading up to our acquisition made this experience the biggest roller-coaster ride of my career.

To me, it was the most positive learning experience in my professional career. But if you think the world of a start-up CEO is always glamorous, then think again. You are completely responsible not only for the direction of your company but also the impact of your decisions on your valued employees. The decisions you make can be the difference in hiring additional employees or terminating the employment of your existing, loyal team. It falls on your shoulders. The margin of error is very small.

People often view careers with start-ups as an exciting way to make a living. In many ways, that is true. But the founders of Involver made many sacrifices, including lower pay and longer working hours, in the hopes of a rewarding exit. The odds are against today's start-ups; most fail to achieve financial success over their tenure. Many never survive the first twelve months of existence.

Salman Ansari, one of the bright and talented engineering managers at Involver, posted this quote by an unknown author on his Facebook page:

Entrepreneurship:
Is living a few years of your life like most
people won't so that you can spend the rest of
your life like most people can't.

Entrepreneurship is defined by Wikipedia as the act of being an entrepreneur or "one who undertakes innovations, finance and business acumen in an effort to transform innovations into economic goods." It is easy to fantasize about being the leader of the next Google or Facebook, but the road to start-up success is never easy. As a start-up entrepreneur, you have to wear many hats and be comfortable with the complexity of running a very diverse business. You have to learn to strive in chaos. You have to be productive in adversity and demonstrate unwavering leadership to your employees. It is easy to become distracted, because decisions from all diverse lines of business eventually fall on your shoulders. You constantly ask yourself: what was the most productive use of my time to benefit the employees and shareholders of my company for that given day?

In this book, I hope to share the experiences of being the president and CEO of a social-media marketing company in the height of the social, open-web craze. Every day brought new, interesting, and many times very difficult challenges. I was fortunate to have two brilliant founders who shared this journey with me.

It is important to note that I wrote this book very much aware that I have signed nondisclosure agreements (NDA) with many of the parties referenced in this book. The content in this book respects the NDA contracts I have signed while at Involver. I have kept all confidential information excluded from the pages of this book. That being said, the stories told here are real, but many names were omitted to respect the confidentiality of others.

This is the story of Involver, a social-media marketing company with a clear vision for our industry, great products, and young, highly skilled talent. Steven Jobs often said to his loyal employees at Apple that the journey was the reward. This too was true with my wild ride at Involver!

CHAPTER ONE

The Opportunity

In April 2010, I received a phone call that would change my professional life in many ways.

At that time, I was the senior vice president of worldwide field operations at Webroot, a security software company located in Boulder, Colorado. I had just left the office of Chris Benham, our chief marketing officer, where we discussed an upcoming product launch. This was no ordinary new product introduction. It was the culmination of significant engineering investments and strategic acquisitions over the past few years.

Our first release of the new product was targeted for the consumer market. Chris and I knew we needed to make the necessary sales and marketing investments to ensure rapid customer acquisition success. We also knew many consumers were spending more and more of their online time on Facebook. We both realized that our company would need to leverage social media for our launch in order to exceed our lofty projected revenue expectations. This was not going to be an easy task, because neither of us had much experience with social-media marketing or the process of gaining website traffic or attention through social-media sites—for example, using social networks like Facebook to advertise and acquire new customers.

Companies were shifting their marketing initiatives and, more importantly, their funding toward Facebook because that is where consumers were spending much of their online time. In recent years, there has been a rapid acceleration of investments in social-media marketing by companies of all sizes. It represents a key marketing mechanism for brand awareness and rapid customer acquisition success. Despite a combined fifty years of sales and marketing experience, Chris and I lacked the knowledge to determine the best mechanism of capitalizing on this emerging trend. Leveraging social-media marketing was an opportunity Webroot couldn't miss; that much we knew. We just didn't know how.

The Executive Recruiter:

I RETURNED TO MY office and was pondering our dilemma when my phone rang.

"Don Beck," I said into my receiver, my mind still swirling around our dilemma.

"Don, it's Brian Kasser from Russell Reynolds," the caller said warmly.

I had known Brian for years and greatly respected his work. After our preliminary greetings, my old friend cut straight to the chase.

"I'm calling you about an opportunity you definitely will want to consider. It is for a position with a high-growth social-media company that needs new leadership to capitalize on a massive market opportunity."

I sat back in my chair and listened to what he had to say, the thoughts of our social-media conundrum momentarily on hold. Brian wanted me to consider being a candidate to be the company's next chief executive officer. While I did have aspirations to achieve this career milestone, my focus was undivided (or so I thought)—the product launch was all consuming. And so I reflexively provided my standard response, as I am fortunate to have reached a point in my career where I periodically received such calls. I expressed my sincere appreciation and concluded, "The timing just isn't right."

He did not give up easily on me. He went on to say, "An opportunity like this doesn't come around very often. This is a very exciting company with two brilliant founders. I know you have a great deal on your plate, but you would be doing yourself a disservice by not learning more about the opportunity. You and I know you are ready for this role and so does Byron Deeter of Bessemer Ventures, who fully endorsed your candidacy for this role."

By mentioning Byron Deeter, a partner with Bessemer Ventures and a man whom I considered both a business colleague and a friend, made this conversation more interesting. I have known Byron for years. His venture capital firm was highly respected and had invested in a previous company where I was responsible for worldwide sales. The company, Postini, was backed by Bessemer Ventures and was sold to Google in 2007 for $625 million. His involvement definitely caught my attention.

I told Brian that I would think about it, but it was unlikely that I would make a career change at this time.

After hanging up, though, the silence in my office was ringing with possibility. It was as if a zap of electricity had shot through the room and everything—my desk, my comfortable office chair, my humming computer screen, and the pen in my hand—was buzzing. This call was different, and everything in me knew it.

I immediately called him back. "Brian," I stated, "maybe you're right. You have perked my interest, and maybe it is time for me to consider this next step in my career. If you would not mind, please tell me everything you know about the company."

"I am glad you called back," Brian replied. "The company is called Involver, which was founded in 2007 and has doubled revenues each year since inception. The company also achieved a great deal, especially in the last twelve months with more than 650,000 accounts (measured by an active public fan page with at least one Involver tab) being powered by Involver. That means that the company was number one in its industry in regards to customer acquisition growth."

His comments were intriguing, but knowing so little about social-media marketing, I could not comprehend the key points he was making about the company.

He continued to tell me more. "The company is located in downtown San Francisco. The San Francisco start-up environment, especially within the social-media industry, is exploding. You really have to experience it to believe it. Young software designers and programmers wanting to work and socialize with other young entrepreneurs are relocating to the city in masses to work for companies just like this one. This company has everything but needs an experienced senior executive to grow the business and to mentor the founders. You are perfect for this role."

Involver was originally founded in Palo Alto but moved to the city to retain and attract new, young entrepreneurial talent. Many of these talented young executives were also being recruited by more prominent start-ups in the city such at Twitter, Zynga, and Pinterest. What I had learned is that start-ups want to be around other start-ups. And because of the significant talent infusion into San Francisco, larger companies began expanding their presence into the city, including Salesforce.com, LinkedIn, Yelp, Yammer, and many others.

I assumed that Involver's growth in customer acquisition was in direct correlation to the increasing acceptance and adoption of social-media marketing. More and more chief marketing officers were starting to view social-media marketing as the most cost-effective mechanism to drive new reach to both a current and prospective customer base. I felt it was incredibly ironic that the very problem that Chris and I were struggling with earlier in the day was the source of an intriguing CEO opportunity for me personally. But based on my limited social-media experience, I questioned how I could be qualified to lead a company so focused on leveraging social-media marketing.

I explained to Brian that I was interested but noncommittal at the moment. I needed to consider if this was the right opportunity for me. Would I have the confidence in my own ability to succeed in this industry sector? Looking back on my career, I had always said that if I never had the opportunity to become a CEO, I would still be satisfied with my career. Nobody believed me, and I am not sure I believed it myself. It was always a career aspiration for me personally, and I knew at fifty-four years of age that time was running out. I might never get this opportunity again. I was very proud of my career's body of work and felt very qualified after thirty-two years of business experience to assume the responsibilities of a CEO. I also believed that I would accept a CEO position if the right opportunity were presented to me.

But Silicon Valley is littered with body bags of failed CEOs who jumped at the first chance for the prestigious title not knowing what they were inheriting. Many of these executives who failed in their first CEO roles are friends of mine. Some have recovered from the experience, but others have not and continue to struggle today. Many of these first-time CEOs made the mistake of pursuing a prestigious title without doing the proper due diligence on the company. Some of these executives failed because they ran out of funding. Some failed because they lacked the experience to be a CEO in the first place. Some just joined bad companies with poor products. The high-tech industry is more forgiving to career risk takers than other industries, but not everybody survives this failed experience. I did not want to make this mistake.

I had some tough questions to ask myself.

- Why do I feel qualified to be the CEO of this company?
- If not now, then when? What career experiences are required to provide me more confidence in my abilities to lead as a CEO?
- If I pass on Involver, will other opportunities be coming in the future?
- If I am selected at Involver, how will I be able to work with the founders?
- How long will it take me to learn the dynamics of the social-media marketing industry?
- How will the employee base react to a CEO over the age of fifty running a social-media marketing company? Will I be able to relate to this young workforce?
- Am I willing to make the necessary sacrifices to run a start-up business?

Before I engaged in the interview process, I had to make an analysis of my strengths and weaknesses and make an honest assessment of myself as a candidate for this role. I have done this skills "gap" analysis my whole career, but if I decided to pursue the CEO role at Involver, it had never been more important. This honest and candid exercise would also prepare me to answer the most difficult interview questions that I was sure to be asked by the founders and the board of directors. I asked myself the following questions:

- What are my strengths, and how does this experience enhance my competitiveness as a candidate for this opportunity?
- Are these skills complementary to those of the founders?
- What are my weaknesses, and will this skill deficit impact my ability to succeed at Involver?
- As a first-time CEO, how can I address the skill and experience shortfall required to succeed as the Involver CEO?
- Am I willing to make all the necessary sacrifices to be successful at Involver?

Coaches and Mentors:

ONE OF BIGGEST STRENGTHS has been the quality of the leadership that I worked for in my career and the lessons learned from these outstanding mentors. As an executive, I have been fortunate to work with some of the best and most brilliant leaders in the high-tech industry. The foundation of who I am professionally was initially established during my eighteen years at IBM. I can't imagine a better institution for learning the basics of business operations and management leadership. My integrity, work ethic, and professionalism were all the result of my time at IBM. I am very proud of my IBM heritage and feel that the lessons learned from this company helped my career advancement long after I left.

I also worked with some of the best thought leaders in the industry, especially over the last ten years prior to learning about Involver. At

Adobe, I was the vice president of North American sales and had the chance to work with both the CEO at the time (Bruce Chizen) and their future CEO (Shantanu Narayen). Both were extremely influential to my development as an executive.

While at Adobe, I remember spending a few days with Bruce on customer calls in New York City. Because we spent the entire day together, he was a captive audience for me, and I took advantage of this special opportunity to ask questions regarding what it was like to be the CEO of Adobe. What were his top priorities for the company? What were his biggest concerns? When did he realize he was ready to lead a company with more than three thousand employees? How did he spend a typical day? This was an experience I will never forget. It also piqued my desires to someday lead a company myself.

From there, I went to Postini, a cloud-based security services company, and had the opportunity to learn from Quentin Gallivan. Quentin distinguished himself prior to becoming the CEO at Postini at VeriSign where he was instrumental in achieving historic growth as the executive vice president of security services. His sales and marketing background was tailor-made for Postini, and we made a great team. Together we doubled the valuation of the company in two years, which led to it being sold to Google in 2007 for $625 million. I am very appreciative of the lessons learned from Quentin and felt he was a major factor in my decision to pursue the CEO role at Involver.

Finally, I worked for Dick Williams at Webroot. Dick had a long and distinguished career starting at IBM in 1965. Since leaving IBM, he has been successful leading numerous companies into acquisition, including Digital Research by Novell, Illustra Information Technology by Informix Software, and Wily Technology by CA Technologies. Dick was one of the most demanding CEOs I have worked for in my career. He expected excellence in every aspect of your responsibilities and would not tolerate missing business commitments. This always brought out the best in me.

I mention these business leaders for a reason. Because of their investment in my personal development, I became convinced I was ready for this next step in my career. Throughout the book, I will reference advice and counsel from these business leaders and how they influenced my decisions at Involver.

Needless to say, I decided to look further into Involver to see if I would be a good fit. I search the web for social-media marketing content and was overwhelmed with the results. This was clearly an emerging technology wave. The high-tech industry goes through computing cycles, and if your timing is right, you can capitalize on a prosperous and profitable run in your career. The sixties and seventies marked the growth of the mainframe; IBM was the dominant company in this market sector. During my years at IBM, I was able to witness firsthand the impact of being in the right place at the right time. I spent most of my career at IBM selling large systems to Fortune 500 companies and greatly enjoyed riding that technology wave. Mainframes gave way to client/server computing where companies like Sun Microsystems became the dominant force in the industry. Then came cloud computing, and my time at the cloud-based security company Postini led to a very profitable exit with the sale to Google in 2007. It was another example of right time, right place.

To me, the social revolution was real and could not be ignored. Businesses of all sizes were turning to social-media marketing and adopting a social strategy that would be a key factor in their ability to achieve new levels of growth, superior support, and customer acquisition. My timing of joining this industry could be very good.

It was becoming clear to me that the social revolution changed all aspects of business, including sales, marketing, product development, and customer support. Employees and customers have more power today than at any time in history due to social media. If customers do not like a product or a company's customer support, they will tell their friends via a social network like Facebook. This viral communications capability can make or break companies. Those companies that have implemented social strategies that permeate all business functions can leverage the power of social media to their advantage.

Despite the trends in social media as the next technology wave, my personal experience with social networking was somewhat limited. I was an extensive user of LinkedIn, a business social networking site where I maintained a professional profile. I even interviewed to be their head of worldwide sales back in 2008. I didn't realize it the time, but I had two LinkedIn accounts. The first one I used almost every day and enjoyed the collaborative nature of this social network. The other had been dormant under an old e-mail address, and I had forgotten it even existed. I heard that they were not interested in me because I did not use their service. I didn't understand what they were talking about, as I valued the LinkedIn network greatly. I did what I could to convince them they were evaluating me on the wrong account but with no success. Needless to say, I did not get the job. The company went public two years later at a valuation of $4.3 billion on the day of the IPO. In my industry, timing in life is everything.

Facebook was another matter. I became curious about Facebook many years ago when my three children used the social network to collaborate with their friends. I went to Facebook and saw that some prominent executives in the high-technology industry had a Facebook presence. I decided to establish my own Facebook page to determine the appeal of the social network to me personally. To my surprise, I had a friend request within the first few minutes of me establishing my page. Unfortunately, it was from the middle linebacker from my son's high school football team. In his profile picture, he was shirtless with his girlfriend on one arm and a bottle to tequila in his other hand. He was also wearing a sombrero. I was horrified. Who would have guessed that my future career path was heading in this direction?

The Company:

DESPITE MY LACK OF experience, I was extremely interested in learning more about social-media marketing and its impact on corporate enterprises. It had become clear to me that senior executives at many companies had come to the realization that they could no longer watch the social revolution from the sidelines. I was convinced that this was an extremely important technology wave and that Involver was a once-in-a-lifetime opportunity.

I embarked to learn everything I could about the industry, as well as Involver. The company had only sixty employees when I first started the due diligence process, but what was more interesting was that it had approximately 650,000 accounts. Many of these accounts were obviously nonpaying customers, and I saw this as a great opportunity to monetize a captive client base.

When I evaluated the company, I had learned the following:

- Revenues were about $6.5 million for the company's latest fiscal year.
- It had grown revenues by 400 percent over the past three years.
- It had surpassed 650,000 accounts or commercial fan pages running Involver applications.
- It was capturing a rate of 2,500 to 3,000 new customers per day via free application downloads.
- It had solid gross margins attainment.
- It had strong renewals associated with its subscription business model.
- One in ten companies on Facebook used Involver.
- Fortune 500 and top-tier agency customers were paid clients of the service.
- Facebook was a paying customer.
- The service was multiplatform: Facebook, Twitter, Google+, Mixi, YouTube, and mobile.
- The client base included 150 enterprise customers (commercial entities versus direct consumers).

Involver offered brands and advertising agencies customizable, automated solutions for their social-media needs. Customers included Facebook itself, the White House, Sony/RCA Records, and Foster Farms. The technology allowed brands to do everything from sharing photos, tweets, and white papers on social-media sites to offering coupons, polls, and even customized landing pages for visitors.

Involver's value proposition (From Wikipedia: "promise of value to be delivered and acknowledged and a belief from the customer that value will be appealed and experienced.") was designed to impact both brand consumers as well as digital advertising agencies. The company provided a social-media platform for managing social communities and campaigns across multiple social networks. With more than 650,000 accounts, Involver powered more Facebook fan pages than any other company. This was an important metric when considering social investments that could attain new levels of customer acquisition.

The company also had very unique intellectual property. Involver created the world's first Social Markup Language, or SML, which allows anyone with basic HTML or javascript coding skills to design Facebook applications. The scalable server-side language abstracts away Facebook social actions using simple tags, enabling developers to create applications more efficiently. In nontechnical terms, this technology was designed to make it effortless and simple to build rich, customized experiences across any social network. Involver's social markup language was proprietary technology that was Involver's lead solution and the basis for the company's growth over the past few years.

Involver also offered a solution called audience management platform (AMP), which complemented the social markup language platform and helped brands and agencies integrate seamlessly with other social-media platforms. Involver's audience management platform is really a social-media dashboard for users, brands, and agencies to manage, monitor, and schedule their appearances on Facebook, Twitter, and the broader social web.

Needless to say, the more I learned, the more impressed I was with what the founders had accomplished at their company. Involver's growth could be attributed to significant industry trends that I felt would continue to positively impact the business in the immediate future. Many industry sources had published articles on how companies were drawing more traffic to their Facebook page versus their web page. This would contribute to the growth of social commerce (sales through social networks) dramatically over the next few years.

A recent Forrester Research article, published July 10, 2009, (http://www.marketingcharts.com/online/forrester-interactive-marketing-to-hit-55b-by-2014-9744/) predicted that interactive marketing in the United States would hit nearly $55 billion by 2014 and would grow at a compound annual growth rate of 17 percent from 12 percent of total ad spend in 2009 to 21 percent over the next five years. According to Forrester's Five-Year Interactive Marketing Forecast Report, search marketing, which composed more than half of 2009's overall interactive spending, will continue to make up the biggest portion of interactive dollars, rising from $5.4 billion in 2009 to $31.6 billion in 2014 at a compound annual growth rate of 15 percent.

In addition to this industry research, I had also learned from Byron Deeter that the company had a product-oriented culture, which is not unusual for an early-stage high-technology company. The majority of the employees were young engineers with a passion for social networking. The company needed additional sales and marketing leadership. The sales team had talent but was also very young and inexperienced. I was considered for the role because I was able to increase sales contributions and grow revenues at previous companies. In the case of Involver, the team was too small to grow revenues substantially, so a major investment in sales and marketing talent was required. I felt very comfortable with this challenge, and with appropriate funding, I felt I could recruit some of the best talent in the industry.

The Founders:

I BECAME A CANDIDATE for this role because Byron Deeter was on the board of directors and had seen me scale a business in the past. Bessemer Ventures was an investor in Postini, and he saw firsthand how we grew the business through renewed sales and marketing investments.

But I was not going to get by the first interview unless I had good chemistry with the two founders: Rahim Fazal and Noah Horton. I went to the company's web page to learn about the founders and their career accomplishments. It is impossible not to be impressed with what the Involver founders had accomplished in their short careers.

Rahim Fazal had achieved a great deal in his short career. Involver represents the third company he has started. *Inc. Magazine* named him one of America's Top 30 Entrepreneurs Under 30. Also, iMedia named him one of the Top 25 Digital Thought-Leaders.

In 2011, he was also recognized by the White House as being one of the top entrepreneurs in the country younger than thirty. Rahim was then invited back to Washington on April 5, 2012, to join President Barack Obama in signing a bill that aims to make it easier for small companies to raise money from investors. He was one of a small number of entrepreneurs invited to witness the signing of the Jumpstart Our Business Startups Act by the president. This achievement was truly a career milestone for this talented entrepreneur.

Rahim grew up in Canada and started his first company while he was in high school. Parents who stressed the value of an education and the importance of excellent grades raised him. But the spirit of an entrepreneur caught him at an early age, and his first start-up was a web-hosting company. This venture represented a significant amount of work for a high-school student. It was clearly a passion for him. Rahim eventually sold the company for $1.5 million while taking his senior-year final exams during high school. Not many people can make this claim.

For his second venture, he then started a web-services platform business and eventually took it public, becoming one of the youngest directors of a publicly traded company in the United States. Again, this is obviously extremely impressive for an individual who had yet to turn thirty years of age.

Rahim epitomizes the word *entrepreneur*, but his career was not the only thing that impressed me about Rahim. As I was learning more about the company, I came across an article in the *Financial Post* written by Tony Wanless and titled "Forget Zuckerberg, how about Fazal?" In this article, he wrote about how Rahim and Noah started Involver and that it was the first company to create a way for brands to use Facebook. The article especially focused on Rahim, who was the youngest student to graduate from the prestigious Richard Ivey School of Business without a prerequisite degree. The article went on to state that together, Rahim and Noah built Involver into an advertising powerhouse.

Noah Horton was also extremely gifted, and his skills were very complementary to Rahim's expertise. Before Involver, he was the software architect for NeoEdge Networks, an in-game advertising business, where he was responsible for developing many of the company's ad products. Noah has held positions at Microsoft, Hewlett-Packard, and Sun Microsystems. At Microsoft, he was ranked in the top 1 percent of the top performers in the company. This was a significant accomplishment and a prestigious milestone for any Microsoft employee. He has filed more than twenty-five patents and published articles on development techniques in widely read publications, including the *Java Developer's Journal*. In September 2008, *Inc. Magazine* also named Noah one of America's Top 30 Entrepreneurs Under 30.

While Involver's board was clearly looking for someone who could scale its sales and marketing, it was also important to bring in someone who was a good cultural fit—somebody who was knowledgeable in many business function disciplines but was also willing to learn from a younger generation. I felt confident that I was a good fit. I realized what I knew based on thirty years of experience, but I also realized what I didn't know and understood that having an open mind would accelerate my learning curve in the social-media industry.

In addition to the founders, it was equally important to earn the trust and confidence of the current board of directors. These were the individuals who invested their money and time in Involver, but most importantly, they expected an acceptable return. Each had broad operational experience and knew what they were looking for with the hiring of a new CEO.

The company was initially funded by angel investors (affluent individuals who provide capital for a business start-up in exchange for convertible debt or equity ownership). These investors provided the required seed money to start the business. Preetish Nijhawan and Neeraj Gupta were managing directors at Cervin Ventures, and together with Alnoor Shivji, a general partner with Global Asset Corporation, they provided the necessary initial funding to Rahim and Noah to launch Involver. All three of the angel investors are self-accomplished executives with both start-ups and established companies. In August 2010, Bessemer Ventures invested in Involver, and Byron Deeter joined the board. The final member of the board was Steve Walske, a highly respected executive in Silicon Valley.

Steve was a major influence to me joining the company. Although I greatly respected the accomplishments of all the board members, I felt Steve would be the most impactful to my development as a new CEO.

Steve is currently a member of a number of prominent boards in the high-technology industry, but it was what he accomplished as CEO of Parametric Technology Corporation (PTC) that stood out to me. He took a company from zero revenues to more than $2 billion during his tenure at PTC. How he did it was equally impressive. PTC had the reputation as an innovator that established an unfair competitive advantage in the market through highly differentiated technology solutions from its competitors. Steve was also a very direct man. You always knew his opinion on a matter, because he was brutally honest. I liked him a lot and felt he could be a great coach and mentor to me as a first-time CEO.

The founders made a very good team, but they fought the idea of having a new CEO join their company. The board members made this very clear to me in the interview process, but Steve was very candid with me.

I had breakfast with Steve early in the interview process. He was very direct. "There's something you need to know," he began.

"Okay," I replied, picking up a pen and a notepad. I could tell from his tone I wasn't necessarily going to like what he had to say, and I wanted to be certain I had all the information.

He continued. "Don, I would be concerned about a major issue before you consider joining Involver. The founders do not want a new CEO and are fighting this board decision. They are lobbying their case with each individual board member. This is not healthy for any company. Whoever becomes CEO must address this issue immediately. The board will not tolerate a divided executive team."

I listened to every word of this conversation. I told him I understood and would consider this point when I meet the founders. After all, they had been successful in growing their business since inception. In their minds, they wondered why a new CEO was necessary. If I were to take on this responsibility, then Rahim, Noah, and I would have to come to an agreement that this was good for the company and that they would both be valued partners of mine in the process.

CHAPTER TWO

The Industry—Social Media Marketing

THE SOCIAL-MEDIA INDUSTRY WAS only about ten years old when I was first introduced to Involver. It was quickly evolving from a youth-oriented methodology of communications and collaboration to a corporate imperative critical for competitive differentiation, which is how a company differentiates its products or services versus the competition.

It was becoming more and more clear that investments in social media must permeate all business functions of a company, regardless of the size of the organization. Companies that can leverage their investments in social assets and infrastructure will establish new and different relationships with their customers. Consumer-product companies will have the ability to better understand the buying patterns of their customers and be able to leverage greater intelligence in reaching and motivating purchase decisions.

Social-media networking brings more power to the consumer. If you have bad customer service, the viral aspect of social-media networks will inform the entire industry. The same goes for bad products. It is now too easy for dissatisfied customers to express their disappointment to the world. But social-media marketing can also be a great mechanism to establish trust with consumers of your products. It can also be a tremendous asset to new product development. I had a great deal to learn about not only Involver but also ever-changing dynamics of the industry.

The Social Media Industry Landscape:

BUILT-FROM-THE-GROUND-UP SOCIAL PLATFORM VENDORS like Involver, Buddy Media, Vitrue, and Wildfire target the social enterprise opportunity. Each of these companies strives to become a ubiquitous independent layer that sits on top of other applications to deliver a single, cohesive experience. Traditional vendors dedicated to enterprise software applications will be socializing their offerings because of the massive business opportunity in the emerging social enterprise. This would make all four vendors mentioned above attractive acquisition targets by the likes of IBM, Oracle, Salesforce.com, Adobe, Google, and Microsoft.

Vendors that can quickly and easily turn on meaningful collaborations for business value (customer acquisition, revenue growth, decreased costs) will have a sustainable advantage in this fragmented, competitive landscape. This is all about business value, not for learning what your friends did over the weekend or where they went on vacation. It is about growing shareholder value. Social investments were quickly becoming the next frontier of competitive differentiation. Involver's importance in the industry would grow in magnitude over the coming years. I was becoming more convinced this was a great business opportunity.

To me, it was becoming clear that web investments no longer provided the business value of the past. Enterprises of all sizes must make the necessary investments to expand their presence in their respective industries by going to where their customers communicate and collaborate. Involver, as well as its competition, helps enterprises of all sizes manage their relationships with their targeted constituents. The social-networking phenomenon could not be ignored.

The market opportunity was also very large when you consider that social media spending was growing 50 percent year over year

($10.3 billion in 2011 to $14.9 billion by 2012). This according to a Gartner press release from October 11, 2011 (http://www.gartner.com/newsroom/id/1820015). Ten to fifteen percent of this spending was tools and technologies to leverage the media spending. This was the total addressable market opportunity available to Involver.

The role of the chief marketing officer (CMO) has significantly changed in recent years. The skills required to be successful goes well beyond traditional corporate and brand-marketing fundamentals. It is critical to leverage the emerging and ever-changing digital-marketing landscape. This plays well for the social-media industry. The CMO's responsibilities are becoming more and more complex. By 2017, CMOs will spend more on IT than the chief information officer, according to a recent IBM advertisement. The CMO is instrumental in aligning the company's values and beliefs with its brand positioning.

Marketers are also under great pressure to deliver results from a multitude of channels. This goes well beyond traditional marketing investments such as print and broadcast advertising, billboards, telemarketing, and direct-mail campaigns. This dynamic was complex enough before, but then you add mobile, social media, and web investments, and it has become a challenging problem for marketers of all size companies. Most marketing executives have limited budgets, and it is their job to place the bets that will provide the greatest return for their employers. Social networks change the game in that they can provide direct customer interaction where traditional channels fall short. The most innovative marketers leverage comprehensive, cross-channel monitoring capability with detailed analytics showing associated return on each marketing investment. A successful social-media marketing campaign should be backed by a complex analytical monitor and reporting capability. Involver addressed this market requirement.

Ad revenue from social networks worldwide was expected to reach $5.54 billion in 2011, according to eMarketer estimates (Techcrunch; October 5, 2011), and would double by 2013. In this analysis, eMarketer took into account a number of popular social networks, including Facebook, Twitter, and LinkedIn. Half of 2011's ad spend on social networks, $2.74 billion, is coming from the US market. Unsurprisingly, the majority of this ad revenue is coming from Facebook, which, at that time, was expected to pull in more than $3.8 billion in 2011 from advertising to its 800 million members. Not many industries could claim this level of growth over the next few years, and I felt Involver was well positioned to capitalize on this market opportunity.

Some additional statistics I researched regarding the market opportunity at Involver got me more and more excited about becoming the company's CEO. For example, it was interesting to learn that according to a study published October 20, 2011, on mobile social-media usage by comScore (NASDAQ: SCOR), a leader in measuring the digital world, 72.2 million Americans accessed social-networking sites or blogs on their mobile device in August 2011, an increase of 37 percent in the past year. The study also provided new insights into how mobile users interacted with social media, finding that more than half read a post from an organization, brand, or event while on their mobile devices (http://www.comscore.com/Insights/Press-Releases/2011/10/Social-Networking-On-The-Go-U.S.-Mobile-Social-Media-Audience-Grows-37-Percent-in-the-Past-Year).

Companies of all sizes are trying to assess how social investments and the company's investment in CRM (customer relationship management) could merge to better serve customers, generate quality sales leads, manage marketing campaigns, and analyze each marketing investment to better penetrate target markets. These investments would be instrumental to any organization striving to enhance its understanding of its customers' buying habits and to align sales, marketing, and support resources most effectively and efficiently. Involver had the technology to build a social experience for commercial clients quickly and easily, enabling new levels of customer acquisition and revenue growth.

Despite these trends, very few companies have social strategies that completely permeate all key business functions across the enterprise. In a recent Altimeter Study, only 43 percent of enterprises surveyed (144 global corporate social-media program managers at companies with greater than 1,000 employees) said they had a formalized strategy road map that addresses how social-media marketing will meet specific business goals. Social CRM has become the new buzzword in the industry, and many large enterprise software companies have made noise that this industry trend will be a strategic investment area for their companies. The rush to integrate social data with function-rich CRM systems can provide a unique competitive advantage for leaders in the enterprise software industry. This technology trend was only just emerging as a business imperative.

Could Involver Capitalize on this Opportunity?

INVOLVER LOOKED TO BE in the right place at the right time. I still needed to assess how well positioned the company was to capitalize on the emerging opportunity that was social-media marketing. I was sold on the industry but had to assess the strengths and weaknesses of Involver.

The company was not profitable, despite doubling revenues every year. A closer view of the profit-and-loss statement showed that the path to becoming cash-flow positive was dependent on growing bookings and revenues dramatically over the next few years and not by cutting costs to a level that would dramatically impact product innovation. The majority of the investment made by the company was in engineering, not uncommon for a start-up at that stage. This was the reason I was considered for Involver. I would be hired to make a significant investment into sales and marketing to stimulate immediate bookings and revenue growth and show a clear path to financial independence. This task did not intimidate me at all as long as we secured the required financing.

In the winter of 2010, Bessemer published the Top Ten Laws of Cloud Computing and SaaS white paper, which was well received in the industry. Its basic premise was that running an on-demand company means abandoning many of the long-held tenets of software best practices and adhering to new operational principles. The document describes the importance of CMRR growth, or committed monthly recurring revenue. In the article, Bessemer recommends using CMRR because it includes both "in production" recurring revenues and the signed contracts going into production. The monthly recurring revenue churn from customers canceling their contracts is also factored into the CMRR calculation. The metric that provides the clearest visibility into the health of any cloud business is CMRR. Having been with cloud-based companies for close to ten years, I embraced many of the perspectives from the Bessemer white paper and used it to assess the health of Involver.

For the two quarters of 2011, Involver grew their CMRR by 130 percent in Q1 and 136 percent in Q2. This growth was very impressive. I was also pleased to hear that the company exceeded its bookings plan for both quarters as well. This meant that sales productivity was exceeding targets, and the sales personnel in the company were making their commissions for achieving their bookings objectives.

The company also had some existing development commitments to business partners, which meant that not all development resources were dedicated to building market differentiating intellectual property. Building integration into partner solutions provided a valuable source of business revenue to Involver, but it came at a cost of deferring key functionality from our product road map. The delivery of requested product enhancements and new features by our valued customers would be impacted by outstanding engineering commitments to existing business partners. This is not to imply that these decisions were wrong. It was a necessary cost of doing business.

Any entity that walks into the doors of a start-up with its checkbook open will get the attention of the executive team. What this means is that these decisions have a trade-off and that the implications of these decisions, both good and bad, must be considered. The benefit of short-term revenue defers the requirements for future funding requirements. That is an important consideration for any start-up. It also means that many aspects of your future product road map may have to be delayed because valuable development resources have been deployed elsewhere.

Involver had thirty-one developers in research and development representing half the employee population. This was one of the strengths of the company. Noah Horton, chief technology officer, and Eran Cedar, vice present of engineering, assembled the team with the vision of building a high-scale, high-reliability social platform in Ruby on Rails and Javascript that would unify the disparate systems that marketers typically had to deal with on a regular basis. Beyond these core skills, Noah and Eran mapped out the development team members with the following unique specializations:

- 40 percent of the Involver development team was focused on highly dynamic Javascript experiences.
- 20 percent of the development team was focused on scale and availability with skills like Ruby language internals as well as automated system provisioning and monitoring.
- 22 percent were experts on the social platforms such as Facebook, Google+, and Mixi (Japan's social network) and have personal relationships inside those organizations. These are people who can call a specific developer at Facebook or Google and get immediate feedback and fixes.
- 30 percent worked on the SML language and have expertise in language design, type systems, schema-less databases, mobile, and partner API integration.
- 26 percent of the organization had people, product, or technical management responsibilities. These people have expertise in lean start-up and agile development methodologies, test-driven development, and traditional management disciplines.

The development team was young and extremely talented. It represented one of the true strengths of the company. Noah and Eran did a very good job of hiring highly skilled engineers and developers.

Retaining this talent was also going to be a very big challenge. Ruby developers were very much in demand by other social-media companies in San Francisco. It was not uncommon to see some of our more talented development resources get competitive offers from other social companies at 20 percent to 50 percent more than their compensation at Involver.

I knew this would be an ongoing struggle. It was important to me that we had the appropriate knowledge-transfer mechanisms in place to ensure the company did not suffer from the loss of key domain knowledge from departing employees. Most technology companies focused on social-media technology have the challenge of keeping their best technologists motivated and incentivized to stay with their organizations. The good news is that the development philosophy at Involver is that everyone needs to code, so managers are also active in the code base and development process.

There was significant competition for young, entrepreneurial development talent. Not only is it critical for companies to offer competitive wages and stock options, but in many cases, that is not enough. Young software engineers demand stimulating work and a work environment that facilitates a balance between work and life variables. This not only means pool tables and Ping-Pong tables being available for breaks but other perks like catered breakfast, lunch, and dinner. While other industries are facing layoffs and union battles, the technology industry is competing for talent, and there is no shortage of perks that can be offered to recruit or retain these employees.

Google started this trend, and it seems every technology company, including Facebook, is trying to top the other with new and innovative incentives for employees to join their company. I joined IBM in the late seventies, and at that time, having an alcoholic beverage on company premise was justification for employment termination. Now it seems every technology company in San Francisco has a stocked refrigerator where employees can reflect on the day's activities over a cold adult beverage. Companies will consider anything to keep the employees happy and prevent them from shopping their talents elsewhere.

The sales and marketing team was young and talented but inexperienced. Most were very proficient in social trends but never had any formal sales training. The very basic concepts of solution selling were missing, but the team achieved success through hard work and being knowledgeable in social-marketing dynamics. Again, this is not a surprise to see in a start-up. I felt I could greatly improve the sales productivity of the team through coaching and mentoring on sales engagement disciplines.

Hiring a new head of sales was also going to be a priority. I wanted to accelerate the hiring of additional sales personnel, and my plan was to hire experienced enterprise sales personnel and teach them social media. I felt it would accelerate their ramp-up time to full productivity rather than hire social-media experts and teach them how to sell. I looked forward to the collaboration of the solid social sales talent already within Involver with some highly experienced enterprise sales resources I was planning to hire.

The sales organization was only ten people spread over San Francisco and New York City. It was a very small sales organization. When you do not have economies of scale, you can't afford any poor performers. When looking back on past sales attainment in previous quarters, I saw a significant dip in attainment from the midmarket team during one particular quarter. When I inquired why the sales attainment dropped during this one quarter, I was told our top sales representative not only got married that quarter but her dog died as well. This was a situation that was very new to me. I never experienced this problem at the large companies I worked at such as IBM or Adobe. It was clear we needed more resources in sales so that I did not have to be dependent on the performance of a few talented sales people to ensure we made our numbers each quarter.

Now, I had done this before and enjoyed the challenge. I had a vast network of sales and marketing resources that wanted to work with me again and learn more about the opportunities associated with social-media marketing. When you have had success in the past and made members of your team money, then it makes it easier to recruit them to new opportunities. I was very proud of my reputation in the industry and knew I could recruit many talented executives from my past to join this incredible team at Involver.

I was convinced that I was about to join the right company at the right time, and I could not hide my passion and enthusiasm when it came to recruiting individuals to Involver but with one important caveat. I made a commitment to myself that I would not hire individuals from my personal network until we secured funding. I wanted to make sure we had the financial resources secured to achieve our immediate goals, as well as to provide a secure career opportunity for my newly hired team.

Again, all this would be predicated on securing needed funding from the venture community.

I could see the potential with Involver and felt I would be a good addition to the team.

CHAPTER THREE

The Interview, Offer, and Negotiation

Meeting the Founders:

IN EARLY 2011, I stood outside the Involver offices on Mission Street for the first time. The thick cloud cover was typical of a San Francisco afternoon, and the crisp chill in the air accompanied my excitement well. This would be my first meeting with Rahim and Noah, and I wanted to make a good impression. My strategy would consist of two key components—showing that I was humble about the opportunity we had before us and being up front about what I brought to the table. While my knowledge of the social-media marketing industry was limited, I had what they should be looking for in their next CEO—the sales and marketing expertise that would take their company to the next level.

Together, the three of us strode the busy streets of the city, settling on a local seafood restaurant for lunch. Inside, after our preliminary exchanges, I asked a question, the answer to which would leave a very positive impression on me.

"I'd love to hear about some of Involver's favorite success stories," I said, leaning back in my chair and taking a sip of black coffee.

Rahim's answer came easily, and it had nothing to do with the large transactions or significant competitive wins I'd expected. It all started when I heard about his friend Vinay who was diagnosed with Leukemia that required a bone-marrow transplant and needed help finding a match. He and his family tried the traditional sources, including e-mail blasts, and were unsuccessful. Rahim heard of this problem and within a week time frame had put together an application that incorporated a YouTube video together with the leverage of Facebook to find a bone-marrow match. This inspiring story was the genesis of Involver and highlighted the power of the social industry. I loved his answer and could see the pride in Rahim when he recounted the story. I also saw a special quality in Rahim's character that impressed me.

I had a long list of questions that I wanted the founders to answer, and I combined them into four major themes

- **Competition:** Describe your competitive advantages over Buddy Media, Vitrue, and Wildfire? How successful have you been in head-to-head engagements? How do you measure win/loss analysis?
- **Culture:** Describe the company culture. Do you experience high attrition? What is your strategy to retain you best and brightest employees?
- **Financial Viability:** What is your cash balance and associated monthly burn rate? What is the time frame to profitability? What is your strategy to achieve cash-flow-positive status? When will a new round of funding be required? How much will be needed? How did you calculate the required funding amount? How will the funding be used to scale the business?
- **Board of Directors:** What is the relationship among board members and their collaboration on key issues? Describe a typical board meeting. How is the chemistry among board members? How collaborative are they in working on behalf of Involver? What are the strengths and weaknesses of the current board?

It was clear that both Rahim and Noah had great pride in their accomplishments at Involver. I also felt the chemistry between the three of us was very good. I shook their hands and thanked them for their time and for lunch. I felt I made a positive impression with the founders and felt they enjoyed the meeting as much as I had.

Walking back to my car, my mind was racing. I really liked Rahim and Noah and felt we could make a good team. I was wondering if they felt the same way. I brought a great deal of experience to Involver but not in social-media marketing. I felt this was a good thing because our skills were so complementary. Did they feel the same way?

Over the next few weeks, I had numerous meetings with both the founders and members of the board, and from these interviews, I felt I was becoming a finalist. I also assumed that the other candidates they were considering were extremely qualified as well. I felt it came down to two qualities that would probably distinguish me from the other executives being considered for this position. The first was my sales and marketing background, which was definitely required at Involver. The second was the chemistry I had with the young founders. I really wanted to work with these social visionaries. I also felt the more I learned about the opportunity, the more I wanted it.

I got very excited about what Involver could become over time. I started selling myself hard throughout the interview process. This process took an extensive period of time that lasted three-plus months. The founders wanted to make sure they hired the right candidate, and I learned later that more than fifteen candidates were interviewed. This became a significant investment of my time, but I sincerely wanted this position.

The Offer:

I was scheduled for a dinner with Byron Deeter on June 2, 2011, and I felt this was going to be the time when I was to be asked to join the company. We discussed a multitude of topics, including what my ninety-day plan would be if I joined the company.

Byron looked me in the eye and asked, "What do you think? Is this something you want to do?"

I was more than prepared with my answer. "Byron," I stated firmly and with a confident tone, "I feel I am a perfect fit to join Involver as the company's CEO. My skills and experience are very complementary to those of the founders, which means I feel we will make a great team. You know based on us working together in the past that I have a track record of growing businesses of all sizes, and I see great potential at Involver. Without a doubt, I am the best candidate for this position, and I look forward to becoming Involver's next president and CEO."

He wanted to hear my personal commitment to the company. There was no hesitation in my answer. Knowing Byron, I also realized there would be no offer unless I exemplified the enthusiasm and passion for the role. It was clear to him that I wanted the position, and I felt very confident in my ability to be successful at Involver. He agreed, and we started to discuss the parameters of the offer. We concluded the evening by agreeing to get a documented offer to me early the following week.

It was late and the parking lot was dark, but I could not wait to call my wife. I had been married for close to twenty-seven years, and she had always been supportive of all my career moves. There was no possible way for me to accomplish what I had done in my career without her support. She is the most important person in my life, and I wanted her to be the first to know that I accepted the CEO role at Involver.

"Suzy," I yelled with an excited tone. "You are speaking to the new president and CEO of Involver. I accepted the position, and an offer is pending over the next few days. I am really excited about this career milestone, and I want you to know this would never have happened without your support."

We had a brief conversation from the darkness of my car in the parking lot. She expressed how proud she was in me and reaffirmed her belief that I would be great as a CEO.

"Let's celebrate this weekend with a special dinner," I stated in the moonlight. I also added that I wanted to tell our children. "Please don't tell the kids. I look forward to breaking the news to them personally." With that, I started the car to drive home.

The Ride Begins:

THE FOLLOWING WEEK I impatiently waited for the call from Byron to discuss the documented offer we had agreed to the previous week. When Wednesday came and went, I finally decided to call Byron to determine the status of the offer letter process. I could tell there was a problem from the tone of his voice. He was looking for the right words to break the bad news to me. After investing more than fifty hours with the interview process, I was expecting a discussion on how fast I could start at Involver. I got something very different.

"Don, something has come up that I have to bring to your attention," he stated firmly but with some hesitation.

I knew this was not good news.

"Although you have been selected to be the new CEO of Involver, there will be no offer because the company has received an unsolicited bid to be acquired. The company will have to go through a due-diligence process to determine if accepting the offer would be the right decision for the shareholders of the company. I know you are disappointed, but these things happen. At this point, it is too early to determine if the offer will be accepted. I wanted you to hear this from me first. Again, if we do not accept the offer, then I fully expect to offer you the CEO position. But for now, everything is on hold."

My disappointment was evident.

"Byron," I stated. "This is very disappointing news. I understand the position you are in and I appreciate your honesty, but from my perspective, I have already joined the company mentally. The thoughts of joining Involver consumed my mind almost every minute of every day since our dinner. I will be honest. I hope the offer does fall through, and then I will have the opportunity to reward your trust in me."

Byron knew the investment I had made and that I had mentally and emotionally left my current employer behind me and was looking forward to this new responsibility. He said that Bessemer Ventures would be supportive of other roles in their portfolio of funded companies for me and that I had his support and sponsorship within his venture capital firm. I appreciated his comments, but by that time, I was completely committed to Involver and felt this was a very unique opportunity that had just slipped through my fingers.

I was convinced that this opportunity was completely gone for me. I expected the founders and the board of directors to accept what I later learned was an acceptable offer to acquire Involver. I realized that this must be a dream come true for the founders, especially Rahim who, understandably, never embraced the idea of a new CEO joining the company. Both had built a great company, and the validation through a successful acquisition exit was a key career milestone for both of them. They also would be rewarded financially because the stock dilution of adding a CEO would not materialize, and their ownership in the company would remain intact.

Byron suggested I stay close to Rahim. He shared with me that these unsolicited offers for acquisition come and go, but without a definitive deal signed by both the buyer and seller, anything could happen. I understood his point, but I did not want to get my hopes up. Rahim and I talked periodically, but nothing really relevant came from our conversations. I just wanted to stay in touch with the founders to let them know my interest in Involver was still extremely strong.

After about two months, I had given up all hope and had focused all my attention on my role with my current employer.

An Unexpected Call:

THE LAST THING ON my mind was Involver when I received a call two months later from Byron stating that Involver had turned down the offer from the prospective acquiring company and was ready to hire me as the company's CEO.

My cell phone rang. When I looked at the caller ID, I saw it was my good friend Byron Deeter.

"I have great news for you," he said in a matter-of-fact tone. "We have decided to turn down the offer to acquire Involver and would like to know if you are still interested in being the company's chief executive officer."

After taking a moment to comprehend what I had just heard, I responded with a simple and straightforward, "Hell yes!"

Then Byron shared some news that was not so good. "That is great to hear. I am glad you still have an interest in the company. You made a positive impression on everybody in the interview process. But there is something you need to know. Rahim had made another attempt to convince the board that he should remain CEO, and out of respect to him, you will need to interview with all the board members again, reaffirming your qualifications and interest in Involver. I think this is only a formality, but it is important next step in your quest to be our next CEO. You okay with this plan?"

Again, I understood Rahim's concern, and I would probably be doing the same thing if I were in his position. I knew this second interview process would be time-consuming, but I wanted the position.

"What choice do I have?" I told Byron. "If this is what it takes to be the CEO, then I am willing to go through the process again. But answer me one thing. Is the board still unified that hiring an outside CEO is still the right direction for the company, or am I competing with Rahim for this position?"

I wanted to be Rahim's colleague at Involver, not a competitor or a threat to him.

Byron assured me that the board was completely aligned with hiring a new CEO but wanted to show respect for Rahim and to listen to his concern.

Rahim and I Become a Team:

THE INTERVIEWS WENT AS expected except for my final meeting with Rahim. I could tell this was to be the final interview of a long and extensive process, and I wanted to really convince Rahim that we would be a good team. Then he surprised me. Out of the blue, he asked me if I would consider a different role than CEO and come on board as the company's chief operating officer. This question told me a lot about the struggle that Rahim was having with a new CEO. I did not want to join the company only to have internal strife with the founders, which always is visible to the employee base.

I made it clear to Rahim that the board was hiring a new CEO and that the decision was already made. He would not be able to convince them otherwise. But I also said that if this was going to be an issue going forward, then I wanted nothing to do with joining Involver. I was completely sincere with my position. This potential internal struggle and political battle would be the worst thing that could happen to Involver, not to mention my own career. This was the last thing I needed or wanted with this new role. He thought for a moment and agreed. We were about to become partners at Involver, and I could not have been happier.

I understood this was a tough issue for Rahim to accept. I told him my thoughts were to have him assume the role of chief strategy officer, and he would also remain as the chairman of the board. We agreed that this was a good approach and shook hands to the future of Involver. He also did one more thing that impressed me.

He wanted to meet one more time over a long lunch not to discuss Involver but to get to know each other personally. This was to ensure we had the chemistry required to be a good team. We talked about our personal backgrounds and family lives. We discussed what we valued in life and what we enjoyed doing outside of our professional worlds. The more I got to know Rahim, the more I really liked him as person. His work credentials and accomplishments were inspiring but so were his ethics and integrity. This last conversation told me a great deal regarding the quality of Rahim's character.

I received the written offer a few days later, and after a review with my attorney, I signed the employment contract and committed to join Involver on September 6. This provided me a few weeks to close out my current position at Webroot and begin the transition process from my current employer to my new role at Involver. The base and incentive compensation offer was far less than what I was making at Webroot, but I had a very healthy equity position in the company. I knew this would be the case if I were to join any start-up, but to me, it highlighted my commitment to Involver and the market opportunity in front of me.

Tough Conversation:

THE NEXT STEP WAS to tell my current CEO, Dick Williams, of my decision. Trust me when I say this was no easy task. Dick Williams values loyalty in his employees. I knew this was going to be a difficult conversation, and I had to be prepared to communicate the logic of my decision.

Dick was very concerned about turnover at Webroot. We were preparing for the most significant product launch in our history, and everybody in the company was working long hours. Every CEO has to deal with this dilemma of employee retention, and the more time you spend with your team, the better you understand how they are feeling and the motivation they have to be a part of the team going forward. Dick was excellent at this task.

One week before I was to inform him of my plans with Involver, Dick and I met in his office in San Mateo, California, and he asked me how I was doing. I told him honestly that I did not know if there was a role for me after the product launch. The product's primary distribution mechanism was to be the online channel, and after spending most of my career in direct enterprise sales, I was not sure my expertise was a match for the new direction of the company. He assured me that my contributions were extremely valuable and I was to be a big part of the company's future. I appreciated his comments, but in my mind, my responsibilities were going to diminish dramatically if I stayed.

I was always a calculated risk taker when it came to my career. I always prioritized the learning experience and the career growth

I would achieve over financial rewards for any new venture. The monetary rewards were always going to be there when my career endeavors made me more experienced and thus more attractive in the market. At that point in my career, I was convinced I needed a new challenge.

The following week I scheduled time to share my thoughts with him regarding my opportunity at Involver. I valued his opinion but also knew this was not going to be a fun conversation with all the work required for the product launch. I was very prepared for the conversation I was about to have with Dick and had a transition plan completely documented and ready to go.

My meeting with Dick was scheduled at the end of the day. I rehearsed my comments over and over in the privacy of my office, knowing that my message would not be well received. I walked toward his office and felt a great deal of trepidation and anxiety.

I sat down in his office and could sense he knew something was up. I didn't hesitate with what was needed to be said and got right to the point.

"Dick, I appreciate your time this evening, and I need to share with you a development that has occurred in my life over the past six months." My heart was racing with each word spoken at this meeting. "Remember when we both joined Webroot? You asked me where I wanted to be in my career and what my expectations were for our relationship together. I said that I wanted you to teach me the details and the nuances of being a CEO and to prepare me for these responsibilities within two to three years. You agreed and said you felt that if I performed, that would be a reasonable time frame. Do you remember that discussion?"

He stated he did remember the conversation.

"At the time, what I was really asking of you was to be my coach and mentor and to prepare me for the challenges and responsibilities of becoming a CEO. You agreed to this arrangement. After two years together, you have more than held up his commitment in this area. Because of working with you over the past two years, I feel very confident that I am ready for this new responsibility."

He looked me dead in the eye and asked without any emotion, "So what are you telling me?"

I explained that an executive recruiter who I felt had a very unique CEO opportunity for me had contacted me. I shared the story on how the Involver opportunity evolved and I had been selected. I acknowledged that the timing was very bad but noted I did not solicit this opportunity. It came to me by a recruiter and a venture capitalist whom I knew and considered a friend. Nobody in the company was aware of this development. Dick was the first to know.

It was important for Dick to realize that this was an opportunity not just to become a CEO but to reinvent myself in the new world of social media, which was quickly becoming the next technology wave in our industry. I then took him through the transition plan I had developed with a member of my management team taking over the responsibilities of demand fulfillment at Webroot.

He was not happy at all. "You realize we are only thirty days away from our new product release? You realize this could not have come at a worse time and that your departure is hurting this company?"

I anticipated his concern and acknowledged his comments. But I explained that I was in my mid-fifties and not getting any younger. I had turned down opportunities to interview for CEO positions in the past and now felt my time may be running out. This could be a last chance to do something that I had always wanted in my career.

He was still not happy and continued to mention how bad the timing was for this development. I never really received his blessing, but after I shared with him my transition plan and recommendation for my backfill, I believed he felt it was a workable plan.

He then surprised me by offering some support. He mentioned that I should have involved him earlier and he could have provided an external assessment of the quality of the opportunity. He noted that his vast experience would have been extremely valuable, but I can't imagine he could have been truly objective knowing the impact my departure could have on Webroot and its upcoming product launch.

This was the most difficult conversation I have ever had in my career. I knew in my heart that if I did not jump at this opportunity, there might not be another one that I felt was this good. As I have mentioned, my whole career I have been willing to take calculated risks as long as I felt I would gain valuable experience in the process. I also knew this would be the biggest career risk of my professional life.

It was also important to maintain my relationship with Dick Williams. I had no doubt that I would experience challenges in this new role where his advice would be greatly appreciated. He was an executive who valued loyalty in his employees, and my commitment to the success of the company could not be questioned or debated throughout my tenure at Webroot.

But it was time for new challenge, and I was ready for what awaited me at Involver.

CHAPTER FOUR

First Days on the Job

Meeting the Team:

RAHIM AND NOAH MADE me feel extremely welcome my first week on the job. We had an all-hands meeting where the entire employee base came to meet me and have an opportunity to ask questions regarding my immediate plans for Involver. During my opening comments, I shared both personal and professional insight on myself as an individual. I described how long I had been married and noted that I had been married for more years than the age of most of our employees. I also mentioned my three children and how much their support meant to me in my professional career.

I then briefly described each step in my career and how it had led me to Involver. I also made it clear that I was very confident that I could make the necessary investments to scale Involver over the next few years. I wanted everybody in the company to know how I looked forward to working with Rahim and Noah and that I was excited to be a part of the Involver team.

I then fielded questions from the employee base. One of the questions was very interesting. An employee wanted to know if I was hired to sell the company. I said emphatically no. I explained that the company did not need me to be sold. I added if that was what the founders and the board of directors wanted then that could be done based on the excitement of the industry and the past accomplishments of Involver. All this could be done without me. The board wanted to scale the business at Involver and felt my background would be instrumental to the success of this endeavor. This is what I wanted to do and saw significant growth opportunity for the company.

Because it was as small company of about sixty-five employees, I expressed my desire to set up thirty-minute interviews with each employee and asked them to be prepared to answer the following five questions:

1. Describe the Involver culture. What makes the company so special from your perspective?
2. What is your background, and when did you join Involver?
3. What are the company's strengths?
4. What are the company's weaknesses?
5. What advice would you give me in my new role as CEO of Involver?

I have to admit that I thought it was going to be fun working with a predominately young workforce at Involver. As I mentioned earlier, most of the employees were younger than thirty, and all were extremely passionate regarding social media. Many of the developers were trained on Ruby, which is a general-purpose object-oriented programming language that provides a very effective and efficient framework for developing high quality code. But it comes at a price. Most social companies seek talented Rudy developers. So to say this skill set is in great demand in Silicon Valley is an understatement. Involver had to compete with the best in social media, including Facebook and Twitter, not only to recruit this talent but also to retain the talent already with the company.

Rahim and Noah did an outstanding job of recruiting great development talent to Involver, including many close friends whom they had worked with in the recent past. But it still represented a significant challenge in scaling our engineering team. To his credit, Noah was very selective in hiring his developers, which made it extremely hard to find the right candidates. It was also difficult to afford this talent. A good Ruby developer straight out of college could dictate a salary in the range of eighty to ninety thousand dollars.

I noticed that we offered breakfast every morning to the employees at our San Francisco office. We were a small company that was tight on cash, and this employee offering surprised me. I realized that companies like Google can offer this perk, but it surprised me that Rahim and Noah felt this was so necessary. When I asked the development leadership team about the breakfast service, they strongly emphasized the importance of these breakfasts as a mechanism for employee retention. I always felt that good pay and stimulating work was enough motivation to retain employees, but this was the social world of San Francisco and I would soon learn that this perk was a relatively inexpensive way to keep employees happy. These breakfast meals were an important aspect of our culture. We tried everything affordable to let our employees know how important they were to the company. Breakfast was a fun way to meet the team in the morning and share thoughts on the company direction over pancakes or eggs.

Throughout the week, I received congratulatory e-mails from my friends and associates within the industry. They all wished me well and gave me encouragement for my future success. No e-mail meant more to me than the one I received from Michael Bennett, the former CEO of SolarWinds.

Michael built an extremely successful company with a unique and innovative business model that started with world-class products and a complete commitment to ease of use for the targeted economic buyer. His prime demand generation mechanism was to offer full-function network architecture products for free and that the success of these offerings would lead to upgrades to their fee-based product portfolio. The more I learned about his company and its success, the more I saw the genius of his business model.

Michael recruited me back in 2007 to run worldwide sales for SolarWinds. The company was positioned for an IPO, but at the time, I just did not recognize how my experience would benefit his company. I told him that directly numerous times—not exactly the best way to get hired. But over time, I continued to track his company's success and realized how much I would have learned by him being a mentor to me.

There was never a senior executive whom I had not worked for directly who had more influence on me than Michael Bennett. I was committed to see a variation of his innovative business model be the basis for our success at Involver. After being announced, I shared these thoughts with him and my motivation to replicate in some way the incredible success he achieved at SolarWinds. He grew his company from $25 million to $150 million in four years, and these accomplishments lead to an extremely successful IPO.

During that first week, he wrote the following to me:

> Great to hear from you Don. And best of luck in your new role.
>
> I have said this to many young or first time CEO's … having done the job for 25 or so years, in so many different types of companies, markets, economies, different investors and exec teams that I have an enormous amount of respect for anyone who takes a shot at it. There is no other role within business where there is no training program to prepare you for everything that is going to come at you every day. And anyone who can take that baton and run the race successfully deserves every $ earned, every praise anyone chooses to offer up, and most importantly, that satisfaction inside that you are a true leader. Satisfaction that as a leader of people smarter than you who you listened to and got out of their way; a leader of people who desperately wanted to be a part of the success but didn't know how so you coached and guided them to be a part of it; a leader of investors/advisors who knew enough to be helpful but not enough to let you do your job so you were able to show them the respect that they deserve as an investor but willing to call your

own shot; a leader of so many people who just want a job so they can pay their bills and take care of their families but don't really want to be out front fighting the fight that so many of us cherish; and to listen to all of them as well as yourself as you call those shots along the way … in those quiet, lonely moments when you will doubt yourself. And in the midst of all this insanity and egos, to remember that it isn't about you and your success … satisfaction that is just a wonderful by product you get for having the opportunity to lead others.

Congrats, best of luck. Next time u get to Austin I would love to catch up.

Throughout my tenure at Involver, I reached back many times and reread his e-mail for motivation.

The first week concluded with a sailboat excursion under the Golden Gate Bridge for all our San Francisco–based employees. It was a great opportunity for me to meet the young and talented employees of my new company in a casual setting. This experience was a great deal of fun. The whole company enjoyed what I guess you could call a booze cruise. The afternoon was beautiful. The sun was shining, and everybody was in good spirits. We departed from Pier 39 near Fisherman's Wharf and cruised around Alcatraz Island with scenic views of downtown San Francisco and the city of Sausalito. It was a true northern California experience, and everyone had a great time. It was also another example of the kind of class and character associated with Rahim and Noah.

Learning the Ropes:

DURING MY FIRST FEW months, I spent a great deal of time with our employees trying to learn what made Involver special and what could potentially be holding our momentum back. I wanted to build trust with the team through being totally transparent and open on all issues within the company. I made it clear that I had a great deal to learn and wanted to have open and candid conversations with all employees. It was extremely clear to me that the employees of Involver were not only extremely talented but also very passionate about the success of the company. It was clear that all respected the founders and what they accomplished by starting Involver. It was also interesting to learn that these employees were not only skilled in their specific business functions but also exemplified strong business acumen. This was impressive.

In my one-on-one meetings with each with the employee, I learned that the strengths and weaknesses of Involver fell into the following categories:

Strengths:

- The company had talented employees who were highly motivated to succeed.
- One of the strongest assets was the company's domain expertise in the field of social media.
- There was an internal culture that was collaborative, energetic, idea driven, innovative, and creative.
- Employees maintained a strong work ethic, and long hours and hard work were embraced.

Weaknesses:

- Renewal rates were starting to deteriorate; customers see more value with competition.
- A lack of required functionality was causing more losses to competition. (For example, analytics and reporting functionality that assessed the status of the company's social-media experience was lacking.)

- There was no sales feedback on current and proposed product functionality requirements for future product development.
- The company was overcommitted and lacked focus on what was really important.
- There was anxiety among employees regarding their future and morale.

These observations did not surprise me. These strengths and weaknesses are typical in early-stage start-ups.

I knew the first year of being a CEO would be challenging, but I felt I had a supportive board, a great mentor in Board Member Steve Walske, and the support of the founders. One of my first hires was Kevin Kunz, our vice president of solution engineering, whom I had worked with at Adobe. I totally trusted Kevin, and he would become a close advisor. I could count on him to always give me a straight answer on our company, as well as my performance as CEO. He was also a very important confidant whom I relied on a great deal on field and product issues.

F8—The Facebook Phenomenon:

DURING THE FIRST FEW weeks of my new assignment I also made learning the dynamics of the social-media market a top priority. For the first few months, it was important for me to spend less time talking and more time listening and learning from my employee base. Our employees at Involver were extremely passionate about social media, and I felt I could learn something from each and every one of them. My first major learning experience was the world of Facebook, and there was no better place for this introduction than Facebook's F8 Conference.

The F8 Conference is held annually in San Francisco, California, and is hosted by Facebook executives. It is designed for developers and entrepreneurs who are building out the social web. All of Facebook's senior leadership is in attendance, including CEO Mark Zuckerberg and COO Sheryl Sandberg.

The term *F8* is derived from the tradition at Facebook for having an eight-hour hackathon immediately after the event. This year's session was held at the San Francisco Design Center, which has limited seating to make the event extremely exclusive. Our company was only able to secure about four tickets, and we heard from many of our agency partners inquiring if we could help them score additional tickets to the conference. Unfortunately, that was impossible. The place was packed. They could have easily sold out the Moscone Center in downtown San Francisco; that would have expanded capacity dramatically. Facebook preferred to make the event very exclusive.

The conference began with a skit with *Saturday Night Live*'s Andy Samberg dressed in a hoody and impersonating Mark Zuckerberg. I had never met the CEO of Facebook before and was seated far enough back in the conference that I actually though it was Mark for a short while and was extremely impressed how humorous he was in his opening comments. After a few colorful jokes, it became obvious that this was the entertainer talking and not the CEO of Facebook.

This conference was quite an education for me. I could not believe the excitement that was generated by the announcements made by Facebook at this event, which included a revamped friend list, a real-time news ticker, and the launch of the subscribe button. But the big news was about the new Timeline. This announcement brought a huge cheer from the crowd. It represented a major recalibration of Facebook imaging of user profiles so that users can see a time-based visual scrapbook of their Facebook profiles. Mark bathed in the incredible positive feedback from his developer community in attendance.

Not being a hard-core Facebook user, I was challenged to determine the true significance of these announcements. I come from the enterprise software world where product announcements are designed to grow customer acquisition or increase shareholder value either by increasing top line revenues, reducing costs, or enhancing internal process optimization. I could not make the connection with how Timeline could grow or improve Facebook's financial position.

Was Timeline key to growing advertising revenues? Would more brands be drawn to advertise with Facebook based on Timeline? I had a great deal to learn.

During the F8 conference, I also had private introductory meetings with Mark Zuckerberg and Sheryl Sandberg. I had a very simple motive for the brief introductory meetings. I wanted to know if they had heard of Involver. I was disappointed to learn that only Sheryl Sandberg had heard of my new employer. I gave both a brief description of the company and let them go on with their lives at the F8 Conference.

I also recognized in the audience Marc Benioff, CEO at Salesforce.com. It did not surprise me to see him at the F8 Conference. His commitment to the social enterprise had been well documented. He saw social-media networking as the next technology frontier and was committed to have his company lead the industry with market-defining social solutions. I was committed to introduce myself and determine if he knew about our company. Involver had built integration with the Salesforce.com solution, so I was optimistic it might lead to a more interesting discussion of greater collaboration between the two companies. Unfortunately, I saw him leave the event, and we never did connect.

After the F8 conference, I had more questions than answers. I made every effort possible to understand how well positioned we were from a product perspective to become a more prominent player in the social industry. Involver had great technology, but could the company be capable of creating a clear competitive advantage in the market?

A Potential Hurdle:

DURING AN INQUIRY INTO our product positioning and industry presence, I learned something that had not come up during the interview process—something that made sweat trickle down my back.

"There is something you should know," said Noah. "But it is nothing you should be concerned about."

I listened quietly as he explained that Involver had been named in a class-action lawsuit. My mind raced as possible implications crossed through it. I asked Noah why I should not be concerned about this news.

"It's not an issue," he assured me, and he seemed very confident in the position. He explained that Involver had been included in the lawsuit erroneously and that our lawyers felt it would be dropped very soon.

I gave him a look of disbelief. "Okay, Noah, I appreciate you sharing this news with me. I will reach out to our lawyers to get their perspectives on our litigation risk," I said in a matter-of-fact tone. I didn't want to overreact to his comments, but this was an issue that could not be ignored.

I reached out to our lawyers who confirmed they were actively involved with the legal process. The feedback from our attorneys was that the lawsuit would be dropped for Involver over time.

I read everything I could on the class-action suit, and although I am not a lawyer, it did seem that Involver was not directly involved in the legal battle. Our lawyers were some of the best in Silicon Valley, and I trusted their assessment of our risk. I did not let it interfere with our plans to build a great company.

Ninety-Day Plan:

AT THIS STAGE, I documented my ninety-day plan, which included a complete list of immediate priorities:

- **Get to know the team:**

  - Assess strengths and weaknesses within the organization; set up one-on-one discussions with each employee within the first ninety days.
  - Gain insight on individual opinions on the company; ensure all voices are heard and acknowledged.

- Compile SWOT (strengths, weaknesses, opportunities, and threats) analysis; gain alignment from all members of the executive team on areas of immediate focus.

- **Company strategy:**

  - Assess the top three priorities for the company for the next twelve months. Establish challenging but achievable goals for each functional line for business, supporting the company's strategic imperatives. Put measurements in place to track our progress.
  - Ensure that strategic clarity permeated the entire organization.
  - Maximize required focus on strategic imperatives.
  - Ensure the reward and incentive system supports strategic imperatives.
  - Determine if we can implement a disruptive business model within our industry that will be difficult for other companies to replicate and have a negative impact on our competitors.

- **Emerging trends:**

  - Can Involver capitalize on these emerging market opportunities?

    o *E-commerce capability within Facebook:* Many retailers are investing in e-commerce platforms within Facebook because shopping at a retailer's website may become obsolete in a few years with the continued proliferation of Facebook users and the expansion of Facebook capabilities. A superior social shopping experience will be a competitive differentiator among retailers. Is there an opportunity here for Involver?

    o *Mobility:* Can we address this critical technology trend that will impact social media?

o *Facebook's deals:* With the recent announcement of deals from Facebook, could it be a mechanism to provide a link to Groupon/Living Social-type offers via Involver. This could represent a link to new target markets and be expanded via mobility capability.

o *Fast-growing entrants into social-media marketing:* How quick can we respond to emerging social-network solutions such as the expected announcement from Google (eventually Google+)?

o *Social-marketing analytics:* Can Involver be the leader in the financial justification of social-media marketing investments?

- **Open issues:**

    - Funding: What will be required to secure the necessary funding to scale Involver over the next eighteen to twenty-four months?
    - CEO mentoring: What is the best way for me to leverage the CEO experience within my network that will help me become a more effective and efficient CEO?

- **How can we improve each functional line of business?**

    - Engineering:

        o What is the product enhancements/priority list today? Are product road map delivery commitments realistic? How can we improve the process to prioritize customer/partner functional requirements?

        o How do the product management, product marketing, and development teams collaborate today? How are feature/function requirements escalated from our customers to the product road map? How are these investments evaluated and prioritized?

o   What investments are required to recruit and retain our best engineering and development talent?

- Sales:

o   What is the capability of the sales team today? What is the productivity per head count within the sales team? What is the average transaction size? What is the price per user? Are these metrics trending in a positive direction?

o   What is the current go-to-market plan and sales coverage strategy? What resources (roles and responsibilities) are required to scale the business?

o   What is Involver's pricing strategy? How does this strategy support the company's business model?

o   Are compensation plans tied to corporate goals and objectives?

o   What sales methodology is used today? Is the disciplined use of the sales methodology a condition of employment within the sales organization? Does it contribute to forecast accuracy and predictability? Is every step of the sales engagement process defined with clear milestones?

- Marketing

o   What is the Involver end-user experience? What investments are required to build the best end-user experience in our industry? Can this investment be aligned with sales and marketing to establish a true demand-generation engine?

o   From a market segmentation perspective, what is Involver's target market, and what is the best mechanism to reach them with our value proposition?

o   What is our competitive differentiator? How can

this advantage be leveraged? What is the best way for Involver to compete in an ever-growing and competitive social-media marketing landscape?

o What is our demand-generation strategy? What is the most cost-effective way to establish demand for the Involver solution? How effective is our search engine optimization investments?

o Is there a formal process for product launches? How often do we introduce new product releases?

o What is our brand-marketing strategy? What is the most effective and efficient way to promote Involver within our targeted industries?

- Technical/Customer Service:

o How is customer satisfaction measured today? Is it trending in a positive direction?

o How do we support our valued customers today? Is it a competitive advantage for our company? Are there more cost-effective means to address customer support in a company our size?

o Are web technical support statistics and trends tracked and leveraged? Is there an initiative in place to minimize the cost of customer support via community and online self-help channels? What investments are required to leverage this cost-effective support channel?

- Finance and Accounting

o What do the financial statements tell about the financial viability of Involver? What are the trends from a revenue and expense perspective?

o Do we have executive dashboards for external reporting to the board? How do we report key performance indicator tracking and financial results? What does the board want to see on a regular basis?

o Is there an established multiyear profit-and-loss statement with funding assumptions? Is there a clear path to profitability? What can be learned from our balance sheet?

o Is there any outstanding revenue recognition issues or concerns?

o What conclusions can be drawn from our cap table? How is the equity of the company distributed among shareholders? Is it fair and equitable?

o What is the trending with DSO (days sales outstanding) and our ability to collect required AR (accounts receivable) debts?

o What is the expense burn rate per month?

o What are the funding requirements and planned use of available capital?

- Human Resources:

o Are performance plans/development plans in place for all employees? Do all employees clearly understand their roles? Are expectations documented with regards to each employee's contribution toward the strategic imperatives?

o What is the onboarding process for all employees?

o What are the company values? Has any work effort been established in this area?

o How can we best recruit and retain talent in the highly competitive San Francisco social-media market?

- Information Technology:

o What IT investments are required? Is the company effective and efficient with IT expenditures? Is there an IT strategy that makes sense for a start-up of our size? Where do we obtain best-practice expertise for our IT investments? How much of our IT strategy should be outsourced?

o   Is our data secured? Is there an information security strategy in place?

o   How do we protect our intellectual property? Do we have patents in place for our key product differentiators?

This is only a partial list of what I needed to learn. I had a great deal of work ahead of me.

CHAPTER FIVE

Operational Game Plan

IT IS EXTREMELY IMPORTANT to any CEO that the executive team is completely aligned with the strategic direction of the company. This was especially important to a first-time CEO. For a small start-up, we had many initiatives going at once. All had their merits and associated business justification, but I was under the impression that the company was overcommitted and did not have the necessary resources to do everything it had planned.

When you lack the necessary resources, you miss business commitments and impact customer/partner satisfaction. It was time to assess what the priorities of the company were and ensure we had the resources to deliver success to Involver. I have always used the term "staff to succeed" when referring to securing the necessary resources to ensure an on-time, under-budget delivery of business commitments.

It was clear to me early during my tenure that we needed to determine where to make strategic investments as a company. We were in a very hot space and had a great deal of investment alternatives that required us to make some tough decisions. The biggest mistake a start-up can make is to try to do too much. We needed focus on the most important investments necessary to grow our business and drive shareholder value. There had been rumblings within the employee base that we traditionally over-committed and under-delivered. It was time for focus.

As a first-time CEO, I was worried about making any strategy changes too soon. I wanted to clearly understand Involver and how we could leverage our strengths in our industry. I wanted to resist the temptation to put my mark on a new strategy. There was too much for me to learn first, and I felt I was surrounded with the talent that would help me understand our strategic alternatives. I also felt it was extremely important to learn how each business function operated and how each function collaborated with other business functions within Involver. I know I was brought on to assist with sales and marketing, but I also made a very conscious effort to invest more of my time in the product and engineering side of the business.

Alignment:

WITHIN THE FIRST THIRTY days of my tenure at Involver, I scheduled an offsite planning session with the senior leadership team of the company. We held the session at Steve Walske's house in Pacific Heights, a very prestigious part of San Francisco. From his back deck he could see the Golden Gate Bridge and Alcatraz on the horizon. It was a beautiful setting for an important meeting.

Steve was an extremely experienced operational board member who had the respect of the entire management team. As an outside business executive to the management team, he was not tied to any ongoing initiative. He could be frank and candid on the direction of the company and ask the toughest questions that needed to be answered.

The goals of the offsite were as follows:

- Agree on key markets and segments.
- Identify key product priorities.
- Gain executive alignment.
- Compile the 2012 plan and funding deck.

Another objective of the offsite planning session was to determine the true value associated with the Involver product offerings. Many decisions had to be made, and most importantly, we needed to be aligned as an executive team on whatever direction we decided for our immediate future.

The Involver leadership team also had other tough questions to answer during this offsite event such as:

In what markets do we invest in today? For example, who is buying our products? What products are customers buying and why? Are customers buying the products through agencies, or do we sell more of our products directly to the brands (companies)? Who is the economic buyer of our solution? Why are they buying the products? How clear is the Involver value proposition? What value are customers realizing? How long does it take for a partner/customer to realize the value? Can the value be quantified (metrics)?

Which market opportunities should we prioritize? For example, what is the size of the total addressable market, and what percentage share do we own now? What is the competitive landscape? Where do we best compete and why?

What are our competitive imperatives? Have we done a gap analysis comparing our solution offering to the competition? Who should we partner with to enhance our competitive position? How well do we compete today?

What is required to go after our selected market opportunities? What will we start/stop/continue, knowing full well we can't be everything to everybody?

The deliverables from this planning session would be a detailed strategic plan to present to the board and potential investors with clearly defined company direction, target markets, measureable milestones, and strategic imperatives that would enable our success.

The first step was to ensure we all agreed on the market trends that would influence the future of Involver. These market trends included the following:

- **Industry insulation:** Social media continues to enjoy insulation from macroeconomic downturn.
- **Increased budgets:** Spending continues to move away from traditional media and into social media.
- **Ad platform integration:** As the above shift takes place, there will be more and more demand for ad platform integration or integrating Involver's technology into a flexible advertising platform for our business customers.
- **Maturity:** As the market matures and invests more in social media, there is increasing demand for analytics and data integration (through conversion).
- **Social CRM:** As brands mature, they are looking for social-media marketing solutions that are comparable to their CMS (content management systems) for their traditional web properties.
- **Tie-in user record:** Brands ultimately want to tie social interaction into their system of user record (e.g., Salesforce.com).
- **True enterprise demands:** As the market matures and enterprises adopt social-media marketing, there will be increased demand for additional functionality for user/page management, permissions, and enhanced analytics to name a few.
- **Platform emergence:** Additional platforms such as Google +, LinkedIn, and international alternatives will continue to come to market.
- **Adjacent players move in:** There is increasing acquisition and extension into the social-media marketing platform space from adjacent industries.
- **Acquisition activity increases:** Acquisitions for technology and referral business will continue to gain momentum

We then embarked on a lengthy discussion about where we needed to place our bets as a company to ensure our future success. We evaluated and debated multiple scenarios and the implications of each investment. We also discussed what would be our competitor's response to our product and go-to market strategy decisions. The discussions were lively and engaging. Nothing was off limits. We discussed the full range of alternatives from simple feature and function enhancements to bet-the-company strategic moves.

I felt Steve was instrumental to the success of these discussions. Steve would say "So what?" a lot during the session when we got caught up in areas where we felt superior to the competition. It was amazing how his two-word questions stimulated so much debate. He forced all discussions on our technology and product developments toward a business discussion on its impact to Involver.

Every investment alternative was evaluated with a **buy** (we buy a company with the current technology, assuming we get the appropriate funding), **build** (we allocate development resources and build the capability internally), or **partner** (we deliver the required capability by partnering and reselling their solution to the market).

From a partnering perspective, we built out our social ecosystem of potential partners from the world of social analytics, customer relationship management, content management systems, and ad management. This was a worthwhile exercise.

We conceptually agreed to do the following:

- **Drive sales resources toward the small- and medium-sized businesses.** The midmarket is a high growth sector for social media. From a sales engagement perspective, the midmarket typically has shorter sell cycles, less dependency on product road map requirements, reduced requirement for professional services, and higher profit margin transactions. We also felt this was an area our competition was ignoring. This also included an investment in more cost-effective sales resources like inside sales teams (outbound phone expertise) versus expensive field sales personnel (direct sales).

- **Focus on our only true differentiator: SML.** This was our sole differentiator as a company, and we decided to make the necessary investments to enhance our proprietary platform for the developer community. As a company, we needed to protect and enhance this advantage and drive adoption with a developer community through enhanced functionality.
- **Deliver a new release of our audience-management platform product to stay in the SMMS (social media management system) business.** Our current publishing, monitoring, and analytic solution lacked key functionality. The decision was made that this solution is required especially with midmarket customers. This would later become a product we called Conversation Suite.
- **Improve analytics to stay in the SMMS business.** Our analytics currently lacked a quality user experience. The data feeds were adequate, but the reporting capability required an investment crucial for selling a social-media marketing solution.
- **Deliver a visual authoring tool.** This investment had to be validated to assess market demand, but the team felt that an application that enabled a quick drag-and-drop capability to build simple social-media campaigns was a potential game changer. This would be built on the SML platform and eventually be delivered to the market as VSML (visual SML).

This meeting was critical in establishing the necessary focus to succeed as a company. Trying to be everything to everybody was a recipe to fail. The renewed focus was also well received by the employees of the company.

A New Road Map:

DURING THE FIRST MONTH of my employment at Involver, we lost two extremely talented developers to another company. I met with each of them before they left, trying to understand why these other companies were more attractive places to work. I had just joined the company, was inspired by the team in place, and felt we had a massive market opportunity in front of us. What did these developers know that I didn't?

Both developers explained very clearly why they were leaving, and it was a very important lesson to be learned at Involver. They explained to me that great developers are true artists. The quality of their work experience is as important as any company perk or compensation plan. They loved working on the next generation of products for Involver that would enhance our competitive position on the market. They thrived on building the next-generation Involver product capability.

But it was explained to me that each quarter a potential deal with a prominent client would become possible for our company to close but only if we could do some custom programming work. This would allow Involver to implement our solution specific to the customer's requirements. Because we were a small company, these resources would be deployed from our valuable development staff that was working on our next-generation solutions. It was described to me as being an artist and going from painting a portrait to painting a barn.

In many ways, we had lost our competitive advantage in the market by committing valuable development resources to close quarterly business transactions and delaying our development efforts toward our product road map. I had heard the same from members of the development team. Rahim and Noah had to make tough decisions as leaders of a start-up, and I never questioned any of their decisions after I joined the company. Most likely, I would have made the same exact decision. Cash flow is vital for any start-up, and it would have been very difficult and challenging to say no to any business opportunity that would have provided valuable revenue and cash flow to Involver. But a clear and concise product road map that would provide product deliverables that would enhance our competitive position in the market was what the company needed at this time.

I called an all-hands meeting for the entire company and had our development leadership share the specific product milestones that would be delivered over the next twelve months. I then stood up and told the audience that anyone who was a developer assigned to these new product initiatives wouldn't be taken off these projects. No potential deal or any business opportunity would distract us from our product development endeavors. We as a company had to be disciplined with this commitment. The message was well received, and the attrition associated with our valuable developers was eliminated, at least for the immediate future.

I felt good about our product direction and the new process disciplines that were planned. Our first with this endeavor was to implement a nonstandard deal-review panel that would meet every week. Kevin Kunz, our vice president of solution engineering and one of the best in the business, would lead this effort. As I mentioned earlier, Kevin was my first hire. We worked together at Adobe, and his thought leadership was instrumental to the success of this endeavor. Also included on this panel would be representation from sales and product management and development.

Now every nonstandard deal would be evaluated on the trade-off between the revenue from the transaction and the potential negative impact on the product road map. All decisions were completely aligned with each business function—no more surprises.

The second was to schedule biweekly sales and product-management meetings to review the product road map and to assess what features/functions were required to close short-term business. This teamwork and collaboration between sales and the product team was important, because key business transactions were sometimes dependent on the delivery of our product road map functionality. This gave the sales organization the confidence to position future capability in order to close currently active sales engagements. It also mitigated any risk from the company's perspective on current and future sales initiatives. We were firmly committed to the product road map, and the development team was accountable for the committed product deliverables. Everyone was responsible for honoring his or her business commitments to Involver.

Revamping Sales and Marketing:

THE IMMEDIATE FUTURE LOOKED bright. One of my top priorities after the offsite meeting was to recruit new sales and marketing leadership to accelerate the growth of our revenues. I knew what type of person I wanted in each role. With the SVP of sales, I wanted a proven performer from my network who had experience in hiring quality sales talent that understood the enterprise sales engagement process. I wanted true sales professionals, and I planned to teach them social media, not the other way around. Because the social-media industry was relatively new, I was not going to find the ten-year sales executive who knew the industry. For this reason, I wanted proven sales performers who wanted to be part of the next technology wave, which was easily arguable to be social media.

This hire was critical to scale the sales organization from ten qualified people to an organization of fifty to sixty qualified and certified sales professionals. To put it into perspective, we went out to LinkedIn to determine how many sales resources our competition (Wildfire, Buddy Media, and Vitrue) had in their organization. Here is what we found:

- LinkedIn showed 165 people in sales and business development (151 sales, 14 business development) out of 310 profiles of people listed as working at Wildfire.
- LinkedIn showed 52 people in sales and business development (11 sales, 41 business development) out of 186 profiles of people listed as working at Vitrue.
- LinkedIn showed 40 people in sales (no business development) out of 217 profiles of people listed as working at Buddy Media.

Involver only had about a dozen sales resources in the company. We were understaffed in sales, but I was very comfortable with the task of building a sales and marketing engine to drive future growth.

My desired qualifications for the sales leader have been the same for the past twenty years. What I look for may not be what others seek in their sales leader. I first look for the ability to recruit a team, preferably from his or her network. The best hires are the ones who have worked for you in the past. In the interview process, I assess the candidate's portfolio of potential team members who will work for that executive again. I also look for process discipline in regard to forecasting and discounting. I always look for consistent performers who are predictable. And finally, I look for leaders who can make good sales personnel better. I look for innovative approaches for training and certification.

The sales role was straightforward in that I knew many in the industry who were qualified to run sales at Involver. Most were with midsize or large companies, and my biggest concern was if they would be successful in a start-up environment. Everyone was excited about learning social media, but working day to day with a very lean start-up takes a different mentality

The Facebook phenomenon was real and gaining momentum. I was confident that with the right sales talent I could teach them how to position social-media marketing investments critical to the success of any sized company. This sales leader had to have the pedigree from some of the best technology companies within Silicon Valley. I would be looking for this executive to bring sales-thought leadership to Involver and deploy best practices within our existing sales organization.

For the position of SVP of sales, I used an eighteen-point evaluation scorecard as follows:

- **Leadership and executive presence:** Does the candidate have the ability to lead and motivate a diverse sales team?
- **Strategic thought leader:** Does the candidate have experience to set clear strategic direction over the next twelve to eighteen months?

- **Operational experience:** Does the candidate have a track record of scaling businesses to new revenue and profit targets?
- **Inside sales experience:** Does the candidate understand the inside sales model?
- **Demand generation experience:** Does the candidate have experience working successfully with marketing to build demand to exceed quarterly targets?
- **International sales experience:** Has the candidate been successful in EMEA or APAC regions?
- **Desire/Interest:** How passionate is the candidate for the sales leadership role at Involver?
- **Problem Solver:** What is the candidate's level of expertise in solving difficult challenges?
- **Cloud/Software as a Service experience:** Does the candidate understand the SaaS/cloud industry?
- **Cultural fit:** Will the candidate embrace the Involver culture?
- **Experience within the midmarket segment of our industry:** Does the candidate understand the specifics of our targeted market segments?
- **Networking strengths:** Does the candidate have the ability to leverage his or her personal network to hire talent quickly?
- **Channel expertise:** Does the candidate understand the dynamics of a channel sales model?
- **Social industry expertise:** Does the candidate know our industry?
- **Sales productivity measurement and analysis:** Does the candidate have a successful track record of forecast accuracy? What process disciplines does the candidate deploy to ensure success with this endeavor?
- **Hiring success:** Does the candidate have a formal process when evaluating new talent? Does the candidate hire successfully?
- **Teamwork and collaboration:** Does the candidate have a proven track record of working well with other business functions?

With each candidate, I had a scale from 1 to 10 to evaluate each category (1 = low experience; 10 = subject matter expert). Different weightings were applied to each category as appropriate to fit the specific sales position. All this scorecard did was to help me with the evaluation process.

When recruiting new talent, especially executive positions, I put heavy emphasis on the reference calls if I am sourcing a candidate whom I have not worked with in the past. I am a very skeptical interviewer. I feel anybody can produce a quality résumé, conduct a great interview, have friends who will be good references, and wind up being an empty suit.

When hiring for any strategic executive position, I have a firm rule. I insist on only talking to references I personally know and respect to gain insights on the merits of the candidate. My best hires have come from me calling an executive I respect in the industry who knows the candidate being considered. I need to know from external validation that the candidate not only did what was documented on his or her resume but also that the candidate achieved these results with integrity and ethics.

The SVP of marketing was different. I needed somebody who understood social media and the dynamics of the industry. This person was to be the social evangelist for our company. This means representing our best interest with a broad base of constituents from industry analysts to public relations firms. The individual needed to know Facebook and its potential impact to not only the business community but society as well. A similar scorecard assessment applied to this hire as well with a greater emphasis on social-media industry experience.

These were my two top hiring priorities. I would also need to secure funding or recruiting any executive would be a difficult challenge.

CHAPTER SIX

Funding Requirement

WITH OUR PRODUCT DEVELOPMENT commitments and growth expectation for the coming year (we projected revenue growth of more than 50 percent with a healthy gross-profit margin) in place, I had a new focus to turn to—securing capital. Armed with these outstanding data points, I was excited to attend an upcoming funding road show and mingle with prominent venture capital firms.

We also decided to slightly reduce our product-development expenses while increasing funding for sales and marketing initiatives to accelerate our growth the following year and beyond. Early-stage start-ups emphasize engineering and development investments to build out their product portfolios. Although more functionality enhancements were planned, our products were solid and well received by the industry. Our emphasis going forward was to scale our business through investments in a sales and marketing capability that would enhance our competitive position in the market. This investment required much-needed funding.

In late September, Bessemer provided a needed bridge loan for $1.5 million to facilitate the funding road show. With a burn rate (the amount of expense money spent each month to run the business) of approximately $300,000 per month, this provided a lifeline into early 2012. This was an expensive proposition for Involver because it required a significant amount of dilution to our share position. All common shareholders would see their ownership in Involver reduced due to this required loan, but it was a necessity to run the business and keep the funding road show active. This was a critical investment because we had approximately 120 days of cash when I joined at the beginning of the month, and we did not want to look desperate for cash when discussing Involver with potential investors.

It was time to get to work. The executive team's top priority was to prepare the presentation content for the funding road show. Byron Deeter and I had many discussions on the importance of me joining the company and adding operational experience and seniority in the funding process. The combination of a thirty-plus-year veteran in the high-technology industry with two social visionaries projected a leadership team that had credibility. This was important because any capital investment would be predicated not only the technology of the company but on the chemistry and expertise of the leadership team as well. Investors needed to feel comfortable that the team in place was capable of building a company that would enable a desired return on their investments.

Six Steps to Venture Capital Funding:

To OVERSIMPLIFY THE PROCESS, typical fundraising from venture capital firms includes the following six steps:

1. An introductory meeting is scheduled with the company seeking investment with the venture capital firm. This could come from a current investor in the company by leveraging its VC network. The company could reach out to the VC community directly with a request for a meeting. Or, the preferred way, the VC could reach out to the company seeking investment because it has heard great things on the company's growth and technology and wants to learn more.
2. An initial brief meeting is held to share the company overview and financial projections expected from a desired investment. Also included in the initial presentation are market opportunity

assessments (total addressable market), company vision, and overall strategy, including competitive intelligence. This is typically done at the VC's office. The presentation deck is most likely e-mailed after this meeting, but some VCs will request it before scheduling the session. The key is to be brief in your initial meeting. Don't overwhelm your audience with too much detail.

3. One of the company executives (most likely CEO) sends an e-mail thanking them for their time and interest and requesting next steps.

4. If interested, then more information is requested from the company. This is a very good sign and is done to educate other partners in the VC firm. This may include second or third meetings.

5. A data room (typically a cloud-based file-sharing capability with secured content management) is established for financial statements and business model information for required due diligence by the VC firm.

6. A partnership meeting is scheduled with all partners in the firm to conduct a more detailed review of the business. This is another good sign, because most companies requesting capital funding do not get to the partnership meeting stage unless there is strong interest in an investment. During this meeting, the company requesting funding does an executive presentation on the company and request for capital. The executive team requesting funding can typically determine the level of interest in an investment based on the detailed questions asked by the partners at this event.

After these six steps are completed, a decision is made to invest or pass by the VC firm. If rejected, then the news will typically come via an e-mail with an explanation for passing on the investment. If a decision to invest has been made by the partnership team of the VC, then the negotiation starts regarding the amount committed to the investment and associated valuation. A term sheet (usually nonbinding and commits the parties to only good faith attempts to complete an agreement to specific terms) is then created to summarize the details of the funding.

A Haunting Memory:

I UNDERSTOOD (OR AT least I thought I did) the risks of joining a company that would need funding within four months. Byron mentioned to me that there was significant interest from the VC community. He had more than twenty-five venture firms who were interested in a potential investment in Involver. I could see the potential of Involver and felt I could make a compelling proposition for investment. I agreed completely with Byron's assessment that this new leadership team would be instrumental in scaling Involver. I also knew I could recruit the talent from my network that would be critical to ensuring the sales and marketing success of the company. I just had to convince potential investors of this fact.

I also remember a very important bit of advice I received from Steve Walske before I joined the company. Steve is an extremely accomplished executive and one whose advice I greatly appreciated and valued.

We were having breakfast at a hotel restaurant in San Mateo prior to me joining the company. I was fantasizing about how exciting it would be to partner and learn from this incredibly successful veteran of our industry when I asked him what should be my biggest concern about becoming the next CEO of Involver. His answer surprised me.

Suddenly, his dark eyes grew even more intense than normal, and he held my gaze. "I don't know why you would consider joining this company without the next round of funding secured. You are setting yourself up for failure. You need to know this is a big risk to you and potentially your career." He stated this in his direct manner.

Wait a minute, I thought. *As a member of the board, shouldn't he be trying to convince me that I would be instrumental to the success of the funding process?* This executive was a huge influence on me joining Involver. This had my head spinning.

He had tremendous credibility with me, but by this time I was completely committed to Involver.

Some six months later, as I began the funding journey, his words played in the back of my mind.

Funding Rounds:

THERE IS ALSO A school of thought around funding. Again, at the risk of oversimplifying financing scenarios, funding rounds are typically associated with certain business objectives. For example:

- **Seed Investment/Series A:** This is generally the first time that company ownership is offered to external investors. This represents the initial funding after seed money to build your business. It typically provides just enough funding to hire the key employees needed to establish proof points that your business has merit and is capable of growing in the near future. Series A financing typically occurs when a company is generating some revenues but usually before profitability. Investors may seek preferred stock or antidilution provisions in the event that additional financing rounds occur in the future. For example, a holder of preferred stock gets paid first if the company is sold. Only after the preferred shareholders of a company recognize their proceeds do common shareholders receive any money.

- **Series B:** This investment is to establish growth to get the company to cash flow neutral if possible. But this doesn't necessarily mean achieving profitability immediately. The purpose of this investment is to establish momentum via well-defined company milestone achievements. Because the company has matured, it will usually have a higher valuation than the previous funding event. You typically see early stage companies reinvest proceeds into the business in order to survive without requiring another round of funding.

- **Series C/D/E:** This is where you invest to scale the business as measured by revenue targets, profitability, or significant customer acquisition. This is a sign you have a very healthy and mature business and that additional funding can achieve market-share growth. This investment is typically associated with the acceleration of go-to market expansion, including sales and marketing investments or geographic expansion. The goal here is to establish a market leadership position to ensure a financially rewarding outcome for all investors.

Typically, the company is revalued before each financing round, so conversion terms may differ dramatically in each round.

Involver's Funding History:

KEEP IN MIND THAT there are many exceptions to these funding objectives. Although Involver had been cash flow positive in previous quarters, it was because of specific large partner transaction had occurred during that specific time period. Profitability when I joined could not be sustained on a quarterly basis without a significant and consistent increase in revenue.

Historically, Involver never had a significant amount of funding since it was founded in 2007. After initial seed investment rounds from angel investors, Bessemer funded a series C round in October 2010 for about $8 million. The press release from October 10, 2010, stated that Involver had surpassed 100,000 customers and closed an $8 million series C funding round, led by venture firm Bessemer Venture Partners. It seemed to me that Involver never had a significant problem raising funding in the past.

Also joining the capital raise were existing investors Western Technology Investment and Cervin Ventures. Rahim was quoted in the press release stating that although Involver had been profitable (He did not mention that it was only in certain quarters where large partner payments were received.), sustainable profitability would not be possible without an influx of cash. He mentioned that this new round would provide the company with additional opportunities to enhance the value from the Involver platform recognized by the company's future and existing customers. Byron Deeter added in the press release that his firm (Bessemer Ventures) had been watching the social web, including sites like Facebook, LinkedIn, and Twitter, turn into an incredibly compelling marketing medium for businesses. He went on to state that there exist very few other venues where brands can interact in such a direct and one-on-one fashion with both existing and prospective customers.

This investment, in conjunction with the angel investment, provided Involver with approximately $10 million in funding, enough to gain some momentum in the industry but not enough to build out a robust product road map and expand sales and marketing to achieve profitability. It was well known that after the Bessemer round, a new round of funding would be required in approximately twelve to eighteen months—right about the time I joined the company. Again, Steve's warning about not joining the company without funding secured was always in the back of my mind.

As mentioned earlier, the first step in this process was to put together the investor deck that would describe the company and how we would use the secured funding to scale the business. The initial funding presentation needed to be detailed enough to catch the attention of the potential investor but leave enough open to secure future meetings.

Our focus was to secure enough funding to last us until profitability. Most venture firms do not give projected financial results from start-ups much credibility. They discount revenue projections because the outlook typically represents best-case scenarios and not necessarily reality. But equally or more important is how expenses would be spent by the executive team. The monthly burn and the cash consumption of the company were of critical importance, and we needed to explain our projections with confidence.

The potential investors also want to see how you plan to spend the capital raised and how you will measure success. We wanted to ask for only what we needed to gain momentum in what was becoming a crowded industry sector. While funding was critical, we also wanted to minimize the dilution of the company's outstanding shares of common stock.

A Green Light from the Board:

ON OCTOBER 3, 2010, the board of directors of Involver met at the Bessemer offices in Menlo Park, California, to get the green light to start the funding road show process.

Rahim, Noah, and I were anxiously anticipating board approval to start the funding road show. We were in Bessemer's boardroom, which can be somewhat intimidating, knowing that many other start-ups had gone through similar experiences, some successful and some not so fortunate. I kicked off the meeting with naïve enthusiasm.

"I want to thank the board for joining us this evening to discuss the merits of a funding road show for Involver. The executive management team is prepared to share our proposed presentation that highlights the requested investment and the associated business plan to grow Involver. At the end of the meeting, I will be asking for approval from the board to start this process immediately."

We presented the funding presentation, and during this meeting, we discussed the merits of every slide and debated suggested improvements to the content. I was pleased that the presentation was well received, and we were encouraged to start the process.

Byron was true to his word in that there was significant interest from the VC community. He knew many of the venture firms interested in Involver, and he would be key to help reach out to the interested parties. He sent out an e-mail introducing me to potentially interested investors with Involver. It was an extremely complimentary e-mail in that he mentioned that I had been "kicking butt" over the past two months finishing out a strong third quarter and building the framework for a successful 2012. He personally encouraged each potential investor to schedule a time for a brief discussion to get to know the company better as we initiated our funding process.

Kicking butt was a bit overstated but much appreciated. The truth was that I was still doing more listening and learning than kicking butt. Byron also provided great advice in preparation for this journey. The entire board of directors were not only supportive but also gave me some valuable suggestions regarding the process:

- *Never* tell one VC firm any of the other names of firms you're talking with until after a term sheet is signed.
- *Never* give them a target valuation. Just give them the post valuation of your last round and note that the company has made a lot of progress since then and obviously hopes to get a "nice up round" this time. Also, we were encouraged to say that we're focused more on the quality of the partner than trying to maximize price. Byron also suggested saying things like, "You guys are the experts on that, so we'll be eager to hear what you think."
- Always suggest you're just talking to a few, very-high-quality firms, you're early in the process, and they're special—you talked to them early.
- Always suggest that this can be a massive, stand-alone, multibillion-dollar IPO story but that you'll be rational if someone comes along and offers a great price along the way.
- Do some homework on the partner before the meeting, so you can say, "We really like you/your firm because of your investment in XX and because YY."
- Don't state a target time frame for term sheets, because then they'll wait until that time and it'll be a negative if you don't have any. Just say that you're at the early stages of the miniprocess but would love to get it opened and closed in Q4 so you can focus on growing the business.

Finding Investors Round One—A Busy Schedule:

GREAT ADVICE. NOW THE ball was in our court, and I was extremely excited to start the process. Both Rahim and I were well known in the investment community. We also reached out to our contacts with key venture firms and scheduled meetings directly to tell our story about Involver.

We planned to start by scheduling smaller VC firms at first where it would probably be a stretch to see them make a significant investment in our company. This was done to ensure our presentation resonated with the targeted audience.

It was also important that the founders and I were well orchestrated in how the content would be presented. I would kick off the presentation with an overview of Involver and why I joined the company. I praised the founders and what they had accomplished at Involver in such a short time. Rahim and Noah were the subject-matter experts not only on the social industry but also on the company, and nobody had more credibility in telling the Involver story than the two founders.

We found a good balance when presenting the content. When I fielded questions on social media or our technology, I would always throw those questions to the founders. The flow of the presentation seemed to work well. Some venture firms were far more interested in hearing from Rahim and Noah, who were truly experts on the social-media marketing industry. Some venture firms were more interested in hearing from me on why a thirty-year veteran of the enterprise software industry would join a start-up in this market space and how I planned to scale revenues. This also included my perspective on the company strengths (product) and areas of required investment (sales and marketing).

We also made the decision to request a $15 million investment and included the associated income statement in the presentation showing the financial impact of this funding over the next three years. Many of the potential investors asked specifically how I was to invest their capital in sales and marketing. I communicated my plan to build out our current sales regions in New York and San Francisco with strong enterprise sales personnel.

I was looking forward to securing funding so that I could get started making some critical sales and marketing hires. I reached out to many talented executives who I had worked with in my past, and almost every one of them expressed an interest in joining me on this new venture. They were all eager to learn about the world of social media. I told them all that once funding was secured, we would work out the details of an employment contract and start building out the best and most productive sales organization in the industry.

During the funding road show, it was important to me to project my confidence that we could scale this business with the right sales and marketing talent and that I could source this expertise from my personal network. This task did not concern me. I had done it before, and I was confident that I could do it again.

During the next three weeks, we conducted initial meetings with numerous venture firms, including Mayfield, Battery, Venrock, JMI, Trident, NEA, Index, Sigma, Globespan, Emergence, and many others. Everyone seemed to understand the competitive landscape of our industry and the fact that the revenue leader was Buddy Media, which had raised $90 million since its inception. It became clear early in these presentations that the venture firms wanted to hear specifically how we were to compete with this well-funded competitor. Involver had only raised $10 million since it had been founded, and this was a concern to potential investors. Buddy Media was not our only competitor. The competitive landscape of Buddy Media, Vitrue, and Wildfire were all companies that, compared to Involver, were all extremely well funded. It was yet to be determined how much this would impact Involver's quest for funding.

The first meetings with the venture firms were simple and fairly straightforward. In some incidents, a junior associate or the partner responsible for the industry sector was in attendance to conduct the initial screening. The VC attendees wanted to know about the company, its competitive position, and the caliber of the leadership team. If done effectively, there would be just enough time for a brief question-and-answer period, and then the meeting would wrap up after about one hour.

Many of the initial meetings centered on the leadership team. This is what the VC was betting on more than anything else. What is their track record in scaling a business? How long have they worked together? How well do they work to collaborate? What are their backgrounds? Do they bring complementary skills to the table? The bottom line to potential investors is to determine if this management team can execute effectively to secure the targeted return on the VC's investment. I felt Rahim, Noah, and I projected great complementary expertise and chemistry.

Some meetings concluded with the VC expressing concern over a conflict of interest with another investment in its portfolio of companies. If Involver competes in any way with another portfolio company, then an investment is unlikely. If this were a potential issue, we still would present our company and solution positioning only and leave out the financial projections. NEA invested in Sprout Social, which is a respected competitor providing social-media management tools to the industry. For this reason, NEA decided to pass on Involver but was interested in Rahim and Noah's perspective of the industry.

Most of our initial meetings were well received. Some concluded with immediate plans to schedule another, more detailed meeting with other members of the VC firm. A few noted that they would get back to us as a way of saying they weren't interested in Involver at that time. I am convinced that a few venture firms only wanted to hear from Rahim and Noah about the industry and their perspectives of future winners and losers in our space. Some sought validation of their current social-media company investments through external perspective from social visionaries such as our founders. Others were kicking tires and were never interested in an investment.

While the funding road show was an ongoing priority, we were also running a business. In November 2011, we were selected as a launch partner for Google+ Pages for Brands and Businesses. We joined five other companies (Hootsuite, Buddy Media, Hearsay Social, Context Optional, and Vitrue). In the press release, Sarah McKinley, Google's product manager, mentioned that we were all selected based on Google's extensive experience helping brands and businesses manage and analyze their presence on social networks. It was surprising that Wildfire was not included in the launch plans. We made this investment knowing it would not generate a great deal of revenue for a long time, but it added credibility to potential investors that our solution portfolio was agnostic to multiple social networks.

The fact that we were in the social industry was enough to present to the most prominent venture firms in Silicon Valley. Many of these firms held investment positions in Facebook and were anticipating a very exciting IPO within a few months. It was fun to debate the merits of Google's entrance into the social-media networking world with its announcement of Google+ and its impact to Facebook's rapid growth. If you were an early venture investor in Facebook, you typically downplayed what Google was doing in social media as a complete waste of time and money. Most venture firms were very opinionated on who would be the leader of the social-network world, and the topic always led to a lively debate. This important partnership with Google+ was also leveraged with every VC presentation.

We received direct feedback from potential investors within a few days either requesting more information or asking for another meeting.

Finding Investors Round Two—Positive Feedback:

AFTER THE FIRST THIRTY days of meeting potential investors, I was still extremely encouraged by the number of second and third meetings that were scheduled. We also continued to have new investors reach out to us every single week. Adding to our list of meetings were prominent firms such as Benchmark, Accel Partners, Redpoint, Venrock, Oak, and Norwest.

Some venture firms were more interesting to us than others based on their investments and commitment to social media in their portfolios of companies. For example, we were very pleased that Benchmark Capital expressed interest because they were early investors in successful social-media companies such as Twitter and Yelp. Accel Partners was attractive based on its success in the market, especially with strategic social-media investments with Facebook and

Groupon. These companies understood social media, and many were involved in funding evaluations with our competitors. These VC firms were very insightful with their feedback to Involver on our position in the market and what was needed to succeed in the ever-changing social-media industry.

Just as VC firms would conduct due diligence on Involver, we did the same on potential investors. This goes beyond their investment portfolios. It is important to have detailed conversations and reference checks on potential board members. Were they supportive during both good and bad times? Was the VC firm committed to the company's success both short term and long term? Will this VC firm be active in helping us scale the business or just look for an adequate return?

Each meeting was immediately followed by an e-mail from me thanking the potential investors for their time and reinforcing our proposal as a quality investment. The e-mails were tailored for each VC participant in the funding road show.

A log was created to ensure we tracked all correspondence with each venture company. We wanted to ensure that all correspondence was well coordinated with each venture firm, leading each of them believe we were more interested in them than their peers in the industry.

I was also impressed with how many of these prominent venture firms knew Rahim. With his recognition as being one of the top thirty entrepreneurs under the age of thirty, it made sense for potential investors to keep track of his career progression. He had also been through this funding process before, and I am sure he'd made a very positive impression in the past.

Some initial feedback was flattering. Here is a sample e-mail that highlighted some of the typical feedback we received from interested venture partners:

Don,

I THOROUGHLY enjoyed our meeting today. Thanks for coming in. It's a very impressive business and, as we discussed, I've found your competitors in the space to have a strategy I think is sub-optimal … not opening up the platform for external developers and creating a healthy ecosystem of 3rd party connectors, analytics, reporting, or sector specialization. Most companies in the space want to own not just the platform but also each module or workflow component. I think your model is closer to what I've been looking for and want to learn more and meet more of the team.

Very much want to push forward on this … can you send me the deck so I can get others up to speed here for the next phase?

I do have some concerns, and you'll find I'm not shy about raising them even at this stage in the process. My belief is that if it's a concern now, raising it can only help both of us reach a conclusion faster - either that it's not a good fit or that it's a good issue and that the type of interaction is valuable. (NOT true for all companies or CEOs … but better for both of us to know that sooner rather than later!)

I think I raised the concerns I already have and email not a good way to discuss them, but I really valued the discussion we had about the sales and marketing to help me feel better about some of those.

This is a very compelling opportunity and I hope we can move it forward on both ends to get to the next phase …

We kept hearing a consistent message about our competition during the funding road show. Although everyone had respect for Buddy Media, Vitrue, and Wildfire, there were perceived flaws in their go-to-market strategies. A good portion of their revenue was generated by professional services. In some cases, we heard that more than half of their revenues were not generated by their intellectual property but in services to customize and configure the social-media experience to the customer's requirements.

I have seen this business model before in the nineties with ERP (enterprise resource planning) software implementations. ERP systems integrate internal and external management information across an entire organization. It coordinates information flow across all business units through an integrated software platform. The complexities of these systems were enormous and required professional services that were sometimes three to five times the cost of the software. Each ERP implementation required extensive manual labor to customize and configure these portfolios of applications to the customer's specifications. As long as your requirements did not change over time, you loved your ERP solution. But what was frustrating to customers is that if your company changed to accommodate changes in its business, and then those modifications would require additional, expensive professional services.

Customers tolerated this business model because they had no other choice for years until cloud-based solutions such as Salesforce.com and Workday offered more flexible and less intrusive alternatives. With cloud-based alternatives, you can implement complex solutions faster and with less expensive professional service requirements.

We tried to capitalize on this position as much as possible by stressing that our product vision provided a very rich social-media experience that did not require extensive professional services. Since our social markup language is a platform that shields much of this complexity from the end user, we felt we had an advantage with our product vision and road map.

Clouds of Disappointment Roll In:

AFTER SIXTY DAYS OF the funding road show, we had approximately twelve VCs interested in follow-up meetings. All we needed was for one investor to commit and provide a term sheet. That would enable Involver to really assess the interest of the investment community. Our current investors could leverage this letter of intent to accelerate any interest from potential VC partners that were interested but noncommittal. Again, all we needed was one term sheet.

There was a healthy sense of urgency with our funding efforts for one primary reason. We were very low on cash. As exciting it was for me to discuss what we could build with some financing, the facts were that we needed an influx of capital to stay in business. We felt we had approximately four months of capital when the road show started. Our lack of cash was very evident to future investors. Without a competitive term sheet, any potentially interested investor could wait us out to secure an attractive valuation for his money. Time was not on our side.

Rahim was my confidant and a person whom I depended on greatly. He was young, but he was also an experienced entrepreneur. He knew the ups and downs of this process. I wanted to make sure he was not discouraged with our lack of progress with securing funding.

Late one night we were both at our desks with nobody around. "Rahim, you okay?" I asked. "You are not discouraged at all from our funding efforts, right?" I wanted to determine where he was mentally. To my pleasant surprise, he was not discouraged at all.

"We are fine, Don. This process takes time. I am confident that we will find the right investor. I am a little concerned but not worried." He confided in me.

It was interesting that I wanted to reassure Rahim that everything would be all right, but he was the one who gave me confidence. He has far more experience from a start-up perspective than I have, and I continued to feed off his experience and demeanor.

Noah, Rahim, and I had been consumed. Now, like the thick fog that rolls in from San Francisco's bay and blocks out the sun's rays, doubt and discouragement began to blot out our early encouragement. Only the intensity of our effort kept fatigue and panic at bay.

Rahim and I split responsibilities by the end of 2011. I would focus on funding, and he would leverage his contacts to secure loan options in case this alternative was necessary. It was becoming more and more likely that we would need alternate sources of capital, because the funding road show had not been successful so far.

As a new CEO seeking funding for the first time, I was surprised that all the early interest in Involver did not lead to a funding term sheet. Analyst reports were being published daily on the positive impact social-media investments could have on corporate America. We continuously modified the presentation to improve our content and messaging around why funding Involver would be a wise investment. I never gave up hope of an investment, but as we approached the end of the year, my optimism was diminishing rapidly. Steve Walske's words played in my mind. Should I have followed a different path home from that breakfast? Given my emotional investment at the time, could I have?

Rahim and I were trying to find answers to why an investment in Involver had become so challenging, especially given that venture capital investments were starting to make a slight comeback over previous years. From 2007 through 2008, the number of active investment funds had diminished each year. This meant that fewer dollars were being invested in technology start-ups during this time frame. This trend continued through the next two years. It was expected to improve in 2011 but only in certain market sectors, such as social media and mobile.

We were hopeful that we would be well positioned to capitalize on this uptick in tech investment. Securing VC investment dollars proved to be more challenging than expected, but we were not alone. We heard from reliable sources that our competitors were experiencing the same difficulties in securing funding for their companies. Social media was a hot industry sector, but investors were being very cautious with their money.

As we approached the end of December, it was time to face the reality that we were not going to secure funding any time soon. We were running out of cash and needed an alternative to a VC investment. After meeting with more than fifty VC firms, we had no immediate prospects that were willing to fund our company. Although VC firms shared different reasons for not investing in Involver, I came up with my own list of five major issues impacting investment. It was clear to me that despite the fact that we were in a very hot industry sector, venture firms were not willing to invest in Involver for a number of reasons. From the numerous conversations I had completed with numerous potential investors, I concluded the following assessment on why we were not receiving any investment interest:

1. Involver was arguably fourth in our industry as measured by revenue. Our competition had more customers, employees, revenues, and funding for future investments. Our solution portfolio or product strategy did not include a disruptive capability that would negatively impact our competition. Without a proven path to establishing an unfair competitive advantage in our industry, it would be difficult to secure funding. Despite the fast-growing social-media market, most investors are not willing to invest in a fourth-place company without a significant competitive advantage or a disruptive business model.

2. Our financial projections (although very realistic) were probably underwhelming to the VC community. We were projecting significant growth of relatively small financial figures. It would take many years to scale to the $100 million revenue target.

3. Based on our revenue projections, a public offering was many, many years away. With this in mind, the only real short-term exit potential was a sale as a result of industry consolidation. Most venture firms did not desire this exit model. Nobody was interested in a short-term flip of a company.

4. Our competition had more momentum both in terms of revenue and paid-customer acquisition. Many of the VCs had talked to senior leadership at our competition who communicated they didn't view Involver as a serious threat to their businesses.

This was humbling. We had a great company with great technology, but we were losing market share to companies that were making the necessary investments to scale their businesses. Rejection e-mails were becoming more prevalent. Most followed the same format as the example below:

Hi Don -

First, thanks for coming in to see us last week. My partners and I very much enjoyed learning about Involver's exciting plans, and getting into a level detail, which exceeded all the great things we have heard about the company.

After some long discussion last week, and a lot more today, I regret to tell you that we're not ready to proceed with an offer to invest in the company right now. In addition, rather than continue to "mull things over" during the holidays. I wanted to share this conclusion with you before the holidays so as to clarify things for you heading into the New Year.

Despite being truly impressed with all the many virtues of Involver, from the customer adoption to the product road map, our main concern remains around the issue of "price point" and all the things that a price connotes within and without a company. As you roll out a lower (sub $100) priced product that will allow for frictionless adoption, we are not clear on how that will integrate with the field sales organization you are recruiting, and so equally unclear on where the center of gravity will be for the product going forward. I dare say that this may not the fundamental issue upon which to focus for Involver in 2012, but it's where we kept getting hung up, and in the end it's precluded us from having a crystal clear vision about which sector of the social marketing landscape Involver will own.

I wish I had better news, and look forward (with some sadness) to watching you build the business in 2012 rather than participating with you. In addition, I will hope that as you grow and prosper that you might need additional capital in the future, and hope that we can intersect with you again at that time.

Rahim, Noah, and I did everything to better understand what the real reasons for rejection were and what we could we do about it. It could be any number of reasons, but the only important fact was that they said no to investing in Involver.

We had to change our course of action, and we needed to do it quickly.

CHAPTER SEVEN

Reality Check

By early 2012, I was becoming more and more convinced that VC funding would not materialize. To Rahim's credit, he came to this conclusion long before I did and tried to convince me that my efforts were a waste of time. Cash was obviously still an issue, and Rahim was working on another bridge loan.

Without a clear path to funding, the only other option was to hire an investment bank and position the company for sale. We had seen the early stages of the industry consolidation with Adobe acquiring a company called Efficient Frontier. The acquisition helped broaden the company's application solution portfolio that was focused on advertising agencies and brands seeking a robust social-media marketing experience. Most large enterprise software companies touted their commitment to the social enterprise or being companies that embrace social technologies throughout their organizations, but no acquisitions had been made outside Adobe to support the company's statements to the industry. We expected that this was about to change.

The Decision to Sell Involver:

THE INVESTMENT-BANKING COMMUNITY HAD been predicting an acceleration of technology merger and acquisitions and pointed to the growing cash surplus of some of the most dominant players in the industry. The additional complexity of a weaker IPO market had encouraged more start-ups to sell when the demand for technology acquisitions is so strong.

Venture partners were also becoming more selective with their investments. David Brophy, venture capital expert and associate professor at the University of Michigan's Ross School of Business, had recently stated in a *Forbes* article titled "What Is Next for Venture Capital" (7/16/2012) that the number of venture capital funds had declined dramatically in recent years nearly down 50 percent from its peak. He drew similarities with the technology hype of the 1990s and what was happening in social media today. He stated there was a lack of evidence or proof point validating its return on investment. Involver, like other social-media companies, had experienced skeptics when it came to financial justification of its value proposition both in the venture world and with commercial customers.

Venture capital firms make the majority of their money not via IPO but through mergers and acquisitions (also known as M&A). According to Dow Jones VentureSource ("Venture M&A Reverses Downward Trend As IPO Market Wobbles"; July 2, 2012), the financial crisis that occurred in 2008 and 2009 basically shut down the M&A market, but momentum shifted in 2010 when $39 billion was spent on 573 deals. In 2011, this trend grew to where $51 billion was spent on 523 deals, and this continued into 2012.

Back in early December 2011, I had dinner with Byron Deeter to share my perspectives on the company and to share with him that the best exit scenario was for the sale of Involver. "Byron,, I said in a concerning tone, "I want you to know that I feel we have exhausted all our funding alternatives, and it is the belief of me and the founders that our only option for a successful exit would be to sell the company. I don't know how you personally feel about this, but I believe this is our only alternative. We are running short on capital, and if you believe that this is the right decision, then we will have to move fast."

He hesitated briefly to comprehend what I had just said. I know it was only a few seconds, but I nervously waited for his reply for what seemed like an eternity. He finally answered, supporting our position entirely.

"I greatly appreciate your support," I said. "To me, it made sense to be proactive and solicit interest from the potential acquires that we felt would be the best partners for Involver and the best homes for our employees."

By this time, we had secured our second bridge loan for $1 million from Western Technology Investment Group. This would provide us the necessary capital but only take us to the end of February 2012. This would not be anywhere near enough to facilitate the sale of the company. Again, a recurring theme for Involver was that we would need more money.

We would require yet another bridge loan in addition to the one secured from Western Technology Investment Group. I made the formal request to Byron at dinner that Bessemer would provide the necessary capital to facilitate the sale. Byron was encouraging but made it clear that we would have to present at a Bessemer partnership meeting and formally request the funding in front of the entire partnership group of the company.

This was not good news. It was clear that if funding was to be approved, it was going to be a decision made by the partnership committee. We would have to present justification just like every other venture investment. The outcome of this meeting could be one of three alternatives:

1. Agree to a bridge loan with favorable terms.
2. Agree to a bridge loan with unfavorable terms.
3. Decide not to offer a bridge loan to Involver and be willing to write off the investment in the company if necessary. We would most likely go out of business with this alternative.

This partnership meeting was not going to be a formality. It would be the most important meeting I'd been part of since joining Involver. The meeting was scheduled at the Bessemer offices in Menlo Park on January 17, 2012. I was pleased to see that Steve Walske was going to be in attendance, because I knew he would provide a balanced and insightful perspective to the session. Although he had not been in my situation before, he clearly understood what we were all going through and provided valuable advice as we approached the meeting.

It was also becoming very clear we would immediately need to hire an investment banker and launch a sale campaign and road show.

I knew that this was the right path for Involver but was still hopeful for a VC investment. Every week a new VC contacted me wanting to hear the Involver story. I kept my hopes alive for VC funding while also preparing for a potential sale. As I continued to meet with VC firms, some actually discussed terms of an investment.

An East Coast venture firm appeared ready to invest up until the partner had a discussion with the CEO of a prominent advertising agency with close ties to Buddy Media. There was nothing specific that was said disparaging Involver other than they did not view us a serious competitor. Again, this was a common theme. That pretty much killed the deal and got me to the point mentally to forego any additional VC discussions. Now I was convinced that funding would not be an option. Enough was enough.

Finding an Investment Banker:

WE EVALUATED A NUMBER of investment banks prior to the Bessemer partnership meeting. Each provided its own perspective on the market and how it would position the Involver opportunity. This included projections of potential acquisition candidates, our value as an acquisition target, and potential valuation for the company.

We also had to negotiate a fair price for the banker's service as well. Some investment banks wanted a flat fee that was extremely large for a company our size. We sought a fee structure that would increase based on the purchase price of the company.

After interviewing numerous investment banks, we selected Morgan Keegan. Morgan Keegan was a leading growth-oriented investment bank with deep technology expertise across all industry sectors. The bank also had a track record of twenty-five M&A transactions and ten equity placements within the past eighteen months. What was especially of interest was the fact that Morgan Keegan was the bank that facilitated the sale of FatWire Software to Oracle. Having firsthand knowledge of completing a recent transaction with Oracle was important, and we felt this experience might pay dividends in the near future. Oracle was at the top of our list as prospective acquirers of Involver.

Morgan Keegan also demonstrated a keen understanding of our industry sector and the dynamics associated with many of our targeted potential acquirers. It understood the social-media market and realized that Involver had the potential to be a market disruptor for a potential acquirer. We had a great deal of value, including

1. a breakneck customer acquisition rate of more than 1 million companies growing at 2,500-plus per day;
2. proprietary social markup language that enabled front-end developers to quickly create and deploy rich social-media marketing campaigns;
3. demonstrated, award-winning thought leadership in advanced digital marketing;
4. large, untapped opportunity to monetize small and medium-sized businesses through Freemium (free product download from the web) offering;
5. a highly scalable SaaS (software as a service) model, rapid top-line growth, and a clear path to profitability;
6. a technology platform validated by partnerships with Facebook, Google+, Klout, and Mixi (Japan's social network); and
7. a disruptive technology platform across content management, social-media optimization, and monitoring.

Hiring an investment banker is not a guarantee for any acquisition success. Rahim, Noah, and I understood that it would be a huge mistake to turn the entire M&A process over to a third party. The investment banker works for Involver but has his own interests in mind. We had no intention to delegate full responsibility for the sale to Morgan Keegan. That is not a disparaging his capability at all. We owned the M&A process, and our investment banker was a valuable asset to leverage.

Between Rahim and me, we had relationships with many potential buyers of Involver, and our active participation in the sale process would be critical to our success. We were a small company, but we felt our books and financial profile were in respectable shape. This was a result of the lengthy funding road show we had completed in 2011. We were ready to put Involver under the microscope. We had flaws like all companies, but we felt we could defend our deficiencies if needed.

Now that we had our investment banker selected, it was time to secure a bridge loan to help us with the capital requirements to secure an acquisition.

The Future of Social Debate:

As we approached the Bessemer partnership meeting, the social-media marketing industry continued to grow dramatically despite mixed signals from prominent players in the industry. To prove this point, just consider the announcements made by Proctor & Gamble and General Motors within a one hundred-day period in early 2012.

On January 30, 2012, P&G announced in the *Wall Street Journal* that it would lay off 1,600 staffers, including numerous marketers, as part of a cost-cutting initiative. This action came from one of the world's largest marketing companies that had an annual ad budget that exceeded $10 billion dollars. The reason for the reduction in staff was a validation for spending ad dollars on social-media marketing. P&G's CEO Robert McDonald quoted to Wall Street analysts that he would have to "moderate" his ad budget because Facebook and Google can be "more efficient" than traditional media that consumes the greatest share percentage of his overall ad budget.

The social-media marketing industry rejoiced at this announcement. Facebook even cited P&G's advertising direction in its IPO filing.

McDonald went on to say that in the digital space P&G found that the return on investment of the advertising, when properly designed and when the big idea is there, can be much more efficient.

Contrast this position to the announcement by General Motors five months later right before the Facebook IPO. On May 16, GM announced in the *Wall Street Journal* that it plans to stop advertising with Facebook after deciding that paid ads on the site had little or no impact on the buying habits of car consumers. This announcement was in direct contrast from the position by P&G and continued the debate over ads on Facebook and how much they helped companies sell more products. GM's announcement occurred days before the Facebook IPO and provided added confusion regarding the projected $100 billion-plus proposed valuation. Many companies advertise on Facebook but do it by establishing free Facebook pages. GM said they would continue this form of advertising versus spending the estimated $10 million annually with the social network.

Small and large companies continue to look for validation that becoming a "social" enterprise was a necessity to compete in their respective industries. These two contrasting views on the benefits of social-media marketing from some of the largest advertisers caused the industry to pause and take notice, especially when the investment world was assessing the value of the upcoming Facebook IPO. How can the social network sustain the 88 percent revenue growth from 2011 when two of the largest advertisers claim dramatically different results?

The Bessemer Meeting:

THE DAY OF THE Bessemer meeting I felt completely prepared. The presentation was very thorough, and Rahim, Noah, and I has rehearsed how we were to present our content. My strategy going in to the meeting was to remind the participants from Bessemer that I was no stranger to their firm.

As I walked into the large conference room at the Bessemer offices, I noticed that the entire partnership team from the VC was in attendance. It was clear that this would not be a simple decision for Bessemer to make, and we had to be very compelling in our position. Steve Walske was also in attendance, and I felt he would be an advocate for Involver.

My heart was pounding as I kicked off the meeting.

"I want to thank Bessemer and the partners in attendance for your time this morning. I also want to thank Bessemer for being a valued partner of Involver. Your investment in our company has been instrumental to our growth, and it is important to express how our partnership is greatly appreciated by our executive team." I was working to set the tone that we had greatly appreciated our relationship with their firm.

Now I needed to get right to point. I continued. "As many of you know, I am not new to Bessemer. I worked with your firm while I was the senior vice president of worldwide sales at Postini where we together built a business that was eventually purchased by Google for $625 million. I felt I was instrumental with Postini in doubling its valuation during my time with the company. The investments I made in sales and marketing helped double the revenue of the company within two years, which was close to $100 million. Bessemer was an early investor in Postini, and it was a very good exit for your firm".

I paused again to make sure this point was emphasized. I wanted the partnership team to know that I felt I was a friend and a past contributor to the firm.

I went on. "I have contributed to your success in the past and feel I can do the same at Involver. A great deal had been accomplished by Involver since our inception in 2007, but the past twelve months we have recognized our most important success across a number of areas including: First, a rapid acceleration of our customer acquisition volumes. Involver has close to 1 million accounts that have installed our SML platform. Free product accounts have grown 447 percent in 2011. Paid customers have grown 268 percent in 2011. Second, bookings have doubled over the past twelve months. New subscription bookings have grown 165 percent, renewal bookings have grown 461 percent, and total bookings have grown 166 percent. In addition, GAAP (generally accepted accounting principles) revenue grew 201 percent ($6.3 million).

"As you know, I joined the company in September as president and CEO to build a business that could capitalize on the tremendous potential we had in our industry. I would not be here without your recommendation and support. Through the funding road shows, we heard consistently that Involver has great products and a strong product vision but lack a sales and marketing culture. Because this is my background, I felt very qualified to scale this business. The team at Bessemer witnessed firsthand that I had done this before at Postini, and you should know that I take pride in my ability to deliver expected results to Bessemer Venture Partners in the past. I have done it before."

I felt my point was well taken. I was not just any entrepreneur off the street looking for another round of funding. I had a track record with Bessemer and felt that point needed to be a part of their decision-making process toward Involver.

I continued my presentation. "In order to capitalize on our unique market opportunity, we pursued an investment round over the past four months, sharing our company's success with numerous venture capital firms, but unfortunately, we have not been able to secure this funding for a number of reasons." I mentioned a few examples:

1. Venture Capital firm's perceptions that social-media marketing will be an area of industry consolidation and that investments in social-media marketing companies at this point would not yield desired results.

2. Funding of competition: (Vitrue at $17 million in February and Buddy Media at $54 million in August) puts Involver in an execution disadvantage. Our planned sales and marketing investments to date were insignificant when compared to the investments of our competitors.

"I need to make it perfectly clear that we have funding that will only take us to the end of February. Forty-five days would not be enough time to facilitate a sale of the company. We have hired Morgan Keegan as our business partner for the M&A evaluation, and together, we have already spent a great deal of time getting their team ready for an acquisition road show. Our banker has already started reaching out to potential acquirers, and the list of potential suitors is growing."

I needed to make another point about Involver and our industry. I also stressed that our industry was only in its infancy. The leader today would not necessarily be the winner tomorrow. Taking away professional services, all four vendors in our space were very close in software revenues. With the right acquisition partner, we would be well positioned to win in this market with outstanding product and a superior product vision. A bridge loan would be necessary to facilitate the sale of Involver, or we would have to consider an immediate plan to shut down the company.

After the presentation, Rahim, Noah, and I left feeling good about our presentation and cautiously optimistic that we would receive the bridge loan from Bessemer. The big question was at what terms. We waited at a local Starbucks for a call from either Byron Deeter or Steve Walske on our fate. Rahim and Noah knew I'd put everything I had into the presentation, but I wanted their validation that I represented the company well in this important meeting.

"How do you think we did this morning?" I asked both men as we waited like expectant parents in a maternity ward. Noah was first to speak. "I do not think it could have gone better. Your opening comments were dead on, and it set the tone for the meeting. I am optimistic that we will hear a positive outcome," he said. Rahm agreed. I felt relieved that my past could be a positive influence on our future together.

We waited. And waited. The longer the wait, the more pessimistic we became. Why was this decision taking so long? We drank our coffee in silence, constantly looking at our phones for a potential text message from Bessemer. I stepped outside for some fresh air. I also did not want the founders to see me worry. It was a beautiful, sunny day in the bay area, but I could not enjoy it. I was consumed with concern over a call that, in many ways, was to save our small company. Minutes seemed like hours. My nervousness grew, and it wasn't because I was on my fifth cup of coffee.

I finally received a call from Steve that we were to receive a $1.5 million bridge loan from Bessemer, but it would be expensive. He did not go into any detail, but it did not catch us by surprise. It was what we expected. We got our bridge loan!

Timing Is Everything:

THE TERM SHEET FOR the bridge loan would still not be received for a few days. During that time, we accelerated our discussions with Morgan Keegan and followed their highly targeted process for acquisition discussions. Morgan Keegan would reach out to potential buyers and discuss the merits of acquiring Involver. Once interest was confirmed, Rahim, Noah, and I would meet with the appropriate parties to tell the Involver story. The level of detail we would share was in direct correlation to the company's level of interest.

The interest in Involver was high because our industry space was tracked so closely in the analyst and trade press. Everything Facebook did was well documented. Any company affiliated in any way to a partnership with Facebook was of interest within the social-media market. It was very good timing to be positioned for sale. Buzz in the industry was extremely high, especially with the Facebook IPO scheduled for early 2012. At Involver, we all thought that the Facebook IPO would be a boost to our valuation.

Facebook filed its paperwork (S-1) for an initial public offering February 1, 2012; the same week the world's largest social network celebrated its eighth birthday. Facebook's S-1 revealed it was looking to raise $5 billion with a valuation estimation in excess of $100 billion. This would mean that the Facebook IPO would be the largest in the history of Silicon Valley. The IPO road show was scheduled in early May and would include the entire Facebook management team. IPO road shows in which company management presents their strategy to prospective investors typically last one to two weeks.

We hoped to capitalize on the Facebook IPO press coverage by meeting with approximately three to five potential acquisition candidates each week. The presentations were similar to the funding road show in that they highlighted the success we'd achieved over the past few years. What was different was that we shared content that stressed what we felt the combined companies could accomplish by joining forces and working together to grab valuable marketing share in the social-media marketing world.

We were excited about the sales process and the prospects for a respectable exit, but similar to the funding road show, time was not on our side.

CHAPTER EIGHT

M&A Process

THE BRIDGE LOAN WAS obviously critical to the acquisition endeavor. A full-blown merger-and-acquisition timeline that starts from initial interest and concludes with the signing of a merger agreement typically takes at least six months. Our forty-five days were quickly dwindling, and we hadn't yet received the term sheet from Bessemer.

We heard from Byron that our presentation was well received and that the Bessemer partnership was supportive of providing the additional capital as needed to support an orderly M&A process. He mentioned that the terms were going to be expensive, but we were not in a position of strength to negotiate many concessions for Involver. He reminded me that this was the second bridge loan that Bessemer had granted, as the first one in September got us through our unsuccessful funding road show.

The term sheet finally came in. Bessemer had gotten us through our unsuccessful funding road show, and the firm would support us now—but the price would be steep. The good news was that we had a viable option. Bessemer was supportive in providing additional capital for up to $1.1 million as long as the angels participated as well to the tune of about $400,000, representing a total package of $1.5 million. This would come at a cost of expensive liquidation preference with any sale of the company.

A Second Option:

AT THE SAME TIME I was discussing the term sheet with Bessemer, Rahim sought out alternative sources of capital that would be less expensive and more attractive. Bessemer encouraged us to do this, because they too wanted the best alternative secured for Involver. Again, time was not on our side, but both Rahim and I had contacts who might be willing to provide loan financing that was more acceptable to the founders and the angel investors.

This is where Rahim's skills as a proven entrepreneur shined. No problem seemed insurmountable to him. Because he had been an entrepreneur his entire career, he was used to quick problem solving. I greatly admired how relentless he was in attacking these challenges for Involver.

Rahim came through with a company on the East Coast called Stillwater LLC, which was the family office of the Sackler family. The company did a variety of public and private lending. Members of the Sackler family are typically in the pharmaceutical industry and are well known in New York City for their philanthropy, donating nearly $100 million a year to various charities.

The terms from Stillwater were acceptable, and the value of the loan ($2 million) was higher than the Bessemer alternative. We did a preliminary comparative analysis between the Bessemer and Stillwater bridge loan alternatives and the specific impact each alternative would have on dilution for the common shareholders of Involver. The board was supported of this alternative but requested more detail on its financial impact to the shareholders if the company was sold. The Stillwater proposal was clearly better across a multitude of variables, and we were motivated to finalize the term sheet.

We needed to finalize and gain board approval for the Stillwater term sheet as soon as possible. The term sheet must be signed in order to have cash in the bank by February 22. This would allow us to make payroll. There would be four to five business days of legal due diligence required to complete the term sheet. Therefore, we needed a definitive decision from the board to execute this term sheet no later than noon on Monday, Feb 13.

We felt that the acquisition process by Morgan Keegan was gaining much attention on the market. The additional $2 million loan would bridge us until the end of June to close a potential sale. It was clear that the best alternative was for Involver to pursue the loan from Stillwater. We secured approval by the board and worked to conclude the final details of the contract.

Desperate Times:

BEFORE BOTH PARTIES SIGNED the contract and the money was deposited in our bank, it was clear that we would not make payroll in time. We had always executed with a sense of urgency because we knew that this was a possibility. Now it had become a reality, and we needed approximately $180,000 to make payroll. Rahim, Noah, and I each contributed $60,000 of our personal money to ensure payroll was met. Nobody in the company was aware of Involver's cash situation, but rumors were prevalent. We downplayed our cash position whenever an employee would bring up the subject. Obviously, we did everything possible to ensure nobody in the company knew we put in our own money to make payroll. I had learned long ago that you never show your employees any emotion, regardless of a good or bad day. Your team feeds off your attitude, and I always wanted to project a positive and optimistic vibe to the company. I did not want any employee to worry about our cash position. Rahim, Noah, and I were doing enough worrying for the entire company.

The monies from Stillwater were deposited, and our personal cash contributions were refunded. We officially had capital to take us to the end of June. During this time, we micromanaged our account receivables to make sure we were getting our payments in on time. I personally made numerous AR calls requesting that we be paid on time. Not often do you think that is the responsibility of a CEO, but these were challenging times and I felt it was extremely important to the health of our company. I felt as the CEO it was my responsibility to do whatever was necessary to ensure the company's financial viability and success.

Rahim, Noah, and I also took significant pay cuts to preserve capital during the sale process. We believed this was the right thing to do for the company. It also demonstrated how committed we all were to a successful exit. The board greatly appreciated this leadership.

We also made the decision not to hire a new sales or marketing leader. We had a very competent sales executive who had great knowledge of the social-media industry. For the marketing void, I hired a marketing consultant from a reputable consulting firm I had used in the past. This provided valuable expertise but did not hurt us too dramatically from a budget standpoint.

In an effort to save cash, the senior leadership team also selected to have our incentive bonuses paid in stock versus cash. This is a common practice with start-ups, but what made this complex with our lawyers was that we were engaged with an investment banker and pursuing the sale of the company. Our lawyers encouraged us not to pursue this practice. It would imply that the founders and I were optimistic about the sale of the company and that this action would benefit us financially more than taking our salaries. We felt we had no choice, so it was recommended that we use our independent auditor, Grant Thornton, to reassess our valuation again.

Grant Thornton replied to our request to validate the valuation assessment done back in September 2011. The company concluded that based on our representation regarding progress of the company since the last valuation assessment, there appeared no reason to update the company valuation at that time. The report cited that the original valuation had taken into account the expected bridge financing. It was also concluded that unless there was a significant change in the operations of the business (new/lost customer, financing, performance to plan, etc.), the current valuation was good up to twelve months. This position would change if a next round of funding were secured or if the company was acquired (nonbinding, binding, or otherwise) or liquidated.

We also felt comfortable that if our action to save money over the past few months by offering a stock incentive program in lieu of cash was ever questioned, then we could show it was done in an honest and straightforward manner.

During this time, some people left our company to pursue career opportunities outside of Involver. We typically did not backfill these individuals because the saved salary was more important than hiring a backfill candidate and waiting for that person to train and become fully qualified. This contributed to the rumors of our poor cash position, so we continued the perception of sincere recruiting efforts. We conducted numerous interviews, but unless the candidate was a superstar, we did not go to offer.

A Reason to Celebrate:

DESPITE THE CHALLENGES ASSOCIATED with funding the company, Involver was still making positive headlines in the market. Another company milestone that we felt would add great credibility to the sale of Involver was *USA Today*'s Super Bowl Ad Meter campaign that provided annual ratings of the appeal of Super Bowl commercials. Consumers could have the opportunity to vote on the most entertaining ads during the Super Bowl while marketers could assess the buzz generated by their ad campaigns. In 2012, *USA Today* wanted to bring the Ad Meter concept to Facebook and capitalize on the viral benefits of the social network.

USA Today partnered with Facebook and selected Involver as its technology partner to create an Open Graph application (The Open Graph protocol enables developers to integrate their pages into the social graph.) that would enable hundreds of thousands of consumers to rate their favorite Super Bowl commercials and share their ratings with friends. Involver focused a significant amount of effort on the user experience and made the Ad Meter campaign extremely easy to use.

The results were impressive:

- 6 million-plus unique users experienced the application
- 200,000 ratings of commercials were posted by consumers
- 2 million video views were driven directly by the application
- 200,000 additional video views were driven by actions that were shared in people's news feeds by their friends who had watched or rated the commercials
- 11 percent increase in visitors on game day to the Ad Meter Page
- 9 percent increase in time spent on the Ad Meter page on game day (to 5.61 minutes)

This was an event that was a source of pride for all Involver employees. We held a Super Bowl party at the office, so we could monitor the activity in real time. We were also pleased that Facebook made it a case study on the power and capability of its social network when deployed in such an innovative way. Obviously, we wanted to leverage this positive press with potential buyers of the company.

The Acquisition Road Show:

DURING THE ACQUISITION ROAD show, a few companies expressed what appeared to us to be strong interest. The two companies we were most attractive to were Oracle and Salesforce.com. Oracle was gaining attention for its push into cloud and social business initiatives. Oracle also had the reputation of being aggressive from a merger and acquisitions standpoint with recent purchases of prominent companies such as FatWire (web experience management), ATG (ecommerce), Endeca (data management), and RightNow Technologies (cloud-based customer service).

Salesforce.com was led by Marc Benioff who had totally embraced the social-media market opportunity and had backed up his social-media commitment with the purchases of Radian6 (social-media tracking), SiteForce (content management system), and Rypple (social performance management). Both Oracle and Salesforce.com were considered leaders in their respective fields and had the resources to dominate targeted markets.

Our discussions with Oracle actually began before I first joined the company. During the CEO interview process, Rahim mentioned to me that he had initial partnership discussions at Oracle. Because I knew many individuals at Oracle, I asked who his key contact the company was. He mentioned Kumar Vora, the SVP of WebCenter Products. I was thrilled to hear this because I had known Kumar for close to ten years, having worked with him for five years at Adobe. Kumar was an incredibly talented and well-respected software executive in the tech industry, and our relationship was close. I leveraged this relationship in the interview process by challenging Rahim to reach out to Kumar as a reference for me. My relationship with Kumar was about to be extended in a very interesting way.

After being selected as CEO, I reached out to Kumar on September 26 to reconnect. We discussed old times at Adobe and how much we enjoyed working together. I acknowledged the fact that he'd had discussions with Rahim regarding a potential partnership with Involver and Oracle. Most of these discussions were strictly exploratory. My message to Kumar was very simple. If there were strong interest from Oracle, I would put all the resources of Involver behind the initiative. But because we were a small company of sixty-five employees, I asked him only to engage with Involver if there was a real partnering opportunity. I could not afford distractions, as I was intent on accelerating the growth of the company and had to focus all Involver's energies on that that endeavor. He clearly understood. He was once a successful entrepreneur of a small company before Adobe, so he could appreciate my challenge.

Throughout the next few months, we would meet on a regular basis, typically once or twice a month. Each time we met I felt the interest in Involver was growing. Kumar was very interested in our funding efforts and how that would impact our strategy. He was confident that I was capable of growing the company if funding were secured. We also shared our opinions on the ever-changing social-media landscape. Kumar was also extremely focused on establishing a social-media product strategy for Oracle.

Our discussions regarding the dynamics of the social-media industry were becoming more and more specific to what our two companies could do together. These discussions were always around partnership, and never did we discuss the potential for Oracle to acquire Involver. I had the same partnering discussions with Google prior to its acquisition efforts to buy Postini.

Rahim and I discussed how we should position the merger and acquisition process with Oracle and, more specifically, with Kumar. We decided that based on my relationship with him, I would have a very frank and candid discussion with Kumar on our funding status and plans for a sale with the assistance of an investment banker.

On December 14, I reached out to Kumar and met him at his Oracle office at the company's corporate headquarters located in Redwood City to relay this very important message. I shared with him candidly that the funding efforts were becoming frustrating. I told him that we were not pleased with the discussions from the venture parties that expressed initial interested in funding Involver and that I strongly believed that the expected consolidation of companies in the social-media industry predicted for early 2012 was hurting our funding prospects.

I spoke matter-of-factly. "So because of what I had just shared with you, the decision has been made to explore selling the company. We have hired an investment banker to explore this alternative. If we like what we hear, we will be proactive in selecting the right partner for Involver. If not, then we will continue to evaluate funding alternatives." I did not want to come across concerned or desperate.

"The sale process would provide a great opportunity for Involver to be proactive with companies that provide the greatest complementary capability to our company today. Oracle is a perfect example." I had hoped to get a reaction from my dear friend.

No reaction at all. He would be a very good poker player.

I told Kumar that Morgan Keegan would contact his corporate development personnel probably after the first of the year to assess the company's interest in Involver. Based on our friendship, I wanted him to hear this news from me personally. He thanked me and suggested that I forward to him the presentation from our investment banker that would be used to highlight Involver's value proposition to prospective buyers. I had an early draft and sent it to him before the holidays.

Exploring the Oracle Partnership:

BASED ON THE NUMEROUS meeting both Rahim and I have had with Oracle, we both felt more and more comfortable that this partnership made a great deal of sense. After the first of the year, I met with Kumar who suggested that Noah fly out to meet with the chief technology officer at FatWire (a company recently acquired by Oracle) who was located on the East Coast. FatWire was a leader in web-experience management and a logical choice to assess the value to Oracle of a partnership with Involver. The idea was for the two CTOs to collaborate on a joint value proposition to see if the two technology solutions could create great business value together.

This type of meeting brings out the best in Noah Horton. He is excellent at assessing from a technical perspective how the two companies could leverage their solution portfolios. Noah returned from the trip east very excited about the synergy between the two companies and with a clear perspective on our potential business collaboration and key partnership advantages, which would include:

- Involver platform bringing FatWire content into Facebook fan pages.

    o This keeps them competitive with Adobe and keeps Oracle ahead of other competitors like Sitecore.

- Involver platform adding stream management to the publishing workflow in FatWire.

    o No one does this well today, and it is a massive opportunity.

- Involver platform adding richer interactive experiences to websites powered by FatWire.

  o Again, no vendor does a great job on this. Most rich experiences are still done by agencies without any platform. Bringing the rich interactivity onto the FatWire platform would be unique for Oracle and would very sticky (making it difficult for a customer to leave you for another competitive alternative). It would mean that all of the agencies working with a customer would be more locked in to the platform rather than operating independently.

  o Involver adding social information about users into the content targeting engine for FatWire. Later, this could also include the ATG product targeting mechanism.

  o Clearly this was the future in targeting. No one did this at all, and no one even had messaging around it. This would put Oracle in the lead.

- Involver platform bringing ATG-powered commerce to Facebook.

  o Commerce on social media was still all experimental at this time, but having the assets of Involver paired with ATG would position us for leadership in the future

This content was to be critical for our next key meeting with Oracle. Kumar set up a very strategic meeting with Thomas Kurian, Oracle's executive vice president of product development. He reported directly to Oracle's CEO Larry Ellison and was responsible for all aspects of product strategy. To prepare for this meeting, we leveraged the knowledge gained from the meeting with FatWire to build a presentation that highlighted the business value of the Involver/ FatWire bundle.

Noah also identified key technology themes for the meeting with Thomas Kurian. We wanted to ensure that all participants in this meeting walked away with three key messages:

1. All of social is media complex. No one was going to become proficient here without a multiyear development effort or an acquisition. Adobe (acquiring Efficient Frontier) was the only company who had made a move here. They were positioned to pull ahead. We could put Oracle into the lead position because we had the best technical product and expertise.
2. The customer benefit was largely around all marketing and e-commerce becoming multichannel, including the traditional websites as well as the new mobile and social-media channels. An Involver acquisition would allow Oracle to enable its customers across all of those channels.
3. This acquisition substantially increased the stickiness of the Oracle offering because it brought all of the agency development done for the customer to be on the Oracle platform. This locked much more of what the customer does in their marketing efforts to the Oracle platform. We felt this would be extremely appealing to the Oracle executive team.

Noah did an excellent job of presenting this content and messaging during the meeting with Thomas Kurian and felt he had a strong connection with the senior executive from Oracle. When we opened up the meeting to feedback or questions, the response from Thomas Kurian was very direct and interesting. He appreciated the prep work that Noah had done for the meeting but wanted us to expand our value well beyond an integrated solution with FatWire.

"I appreciate your preparation for this meeting, and you are right that integration with FatWire is important. But that is only the beginning of what we are building here at Oracle," he said in a very direct manner.

I could tell that Thomas was a man who did not like wasting his time.

He continued, "As you know, Oracle had completed a number of strategic acquisitions, including Endeca, RightNow Technologies, and ATG, and our solution would have to leverage the entire application stack that Oracle was building."

Thomas was extremely insightful to what he wanted to build at Oracle and was going to be aggressive with any acquisition decision that would accelerate Oracle's time to market.

Noah and Thomas shared a similar vision. Both felt the leaders of social-media marketing would need to build a complete end-to-end solution far outside the scope of what Involver or any other company had built to date. What Thomas described was exactly what Noah felt the market was demanding. Noah left the meeting enamored with what he'd heard and kept saying how he would enjoy working for a software executive with such vision.

"I would love to work for that guy!" Noah said emphatically. "I am blown away by his vision. He said many of the things I have been saying regarding what it will take to win in the social industry. He gets it. He really gets it."

I too walked out excited about the prospects of a joint value proposition with Oracle, but I was equally cautious and concerned. "Noah," I asked. "But what if they buy one of our competitors? They will be building this vision without us. How will we be able to compete at an independent company?"

He had no answer. I did not want to kill the moment, but the reality of this possibility could not be ignored.

The meeting with Thomas Kurian proved to be successful in that additional meetings were immediately scheduled over the next few weeks. Oracle wanted to do more technical due diligence on our products, so the next step was to share our technology story with the CTOs of the companies recently acquired by Oracle. The founders and I were thrilled!

The CTO meeting with Oracle was a defining moment with our proposed acquisition with Oracle. We had to convince the technical leadership of Oracle that we would be a good fit for the company and that it would make more sense for Oracle to buy us versus build this capability internally. We knew Oracle lacked social-media engineering talent and hoped they were leaning toward an acquisition.

The meeting was scheduled for March 14, 2012. Besides our business sponsor, Kumar Vora, we had in attendance the CTOs from each of the companies Oracle had recently acquired. In attendance were CTOs from ATG (acquired November 2010), FatWire (acquired June 2011), RightNow Technologies (acquired October 2011), and Endeca (also acquired October 2011). It was clear that everybody invited by Oracle had done his homework and wanted to skip the company overview and jump right into the technology content and product demonstrations. We knew this was to be a very technical session, so to make sure we were able to address all their issues; we invited key members of our engineering team.

By inviting key members of the engineering team to the Oracle meeting, we knew they would quickly figure out that this meeting was about a potential acquisition. We handpicked the employees from Involver who would attend this session based on their technical expertise and professionalism. We settled on Eran Cedar (VP of engineering), Salman Ansari (engineering manager and one of Involver's early hires), and Rehan Ifitkhar (program manager). This was definitely the A team, and I was extremely confident that Involver would be represented well in this session. I also trusted them to keep these meetings a secret with the employee base of Involver.

The meeting lasted five hours. The interaction was outstanding, and the chemistry between all participants was extremely encouraging. I felt that the meeting ended very well when questions shifted away from our technology/solution offerings to the market opportunity and what it would take to capture market share together. We left Oracle feeling very good.

We stopped by a local steak house and had a round of beers to debrief on the events of the day and to celebrate a major milestone in the history of Involver. It was a dark bar, and we took the table in the back because we were close to the Oracle campus and did not want any potential Oracle executives to hear our conversation. Although no commitment was made at this meeting, I felt Oracle had to be extremely impressed with the technical talent of the Involver team.

"Guys," I said. "I am very optimistic. This team made Involver very proud today. Each of you had immense credibility with their technical team. I could not be more pleased. I hope you all feel the same way. Today was a great day for Involver."

They all agreed that it had been a fantastic meeting. I then reminded them, "Please remember that the meeting we just had is highly confidential, and I don't want any rumors being spread at our office. I trust each of you and know that we will not be discussing this meeting or any next steps with anybody outside of who is sitting at our table. Agreed?"

Everyone agreed in unison. Another reason to feel great for Involver and our potential future with Oracle.

Another Distraction:

A MONTH AFTER THE CTO meeting with Oracle, another interesting and unanticipated development occurred as we continued to have acquisition discussions with Oracle. Our investment banker was sold, and the personnel assigned to the Involver sale were not going to be with the acquiring company. Morgan Keegan was sold to Raymond James on Friday, April 13. As a result, the Morgan Keegan Technology Group was officially shut down. Our prime investment banker joined Shea & Co., which is a Boston-based software/SaaS boutique. Other members of the former Morgan Keegan team working to sell Involver joined Signal Hill, which is another boutique investment bank.

Rahim came into our office in San Francisco and told me he had something to share with me privately. It was clear this was not good news, but by this time, I was pretty much numb to any more bad news. It happened so frequently that it was almost expected. We always found a way to minimize its impact to Involver.

"What is it now?" I said with a smile.

"I just heard that our investment banker was sold and that the team supporting our M&A activity is dissolving," he said with concern in his eyes.

I shook my head in disbelief and said, "Another bump in the road. We will survive this issue as well. Let's get on the phone with our former investment bankers to determine next steps."

To say this was a distraction was an understatement. We had put a great deal of trust and confidence with our team at Morgan Keegan, and this came as a big surprise. The members of the investment banking team did not anticipate they were going to be acquired during our sale process, and I held no ill feelings toward the team at Morgan Keegan. But it was clearly understandable that they would be more worried about their own personal outcome and future employment than the immediate future for the team at Involver. I would say I was more frustrated than upset, but it highlighted the importance of not delegating the full responsibility of selling your company to any third party.

Getting in the Door with Salesforce.com:

THE ROLLER-COASTER RIDE ASSOCIATED with Involver had to be experienced firsthand to be believed. Rahim, Noah, and I were frustrated by this development, but it did not deter our belief that a successful exit through acquisition was a real possibility.

Despite acquisition interest from a number of companies, we were surprised that there seemed little interest from Salesforce.com. This was also concerning because we were hearing rumors that the company was potentially going to acquire Buddy Media. (We first heard this rumor at a Facebook event in New York City back in late February.) We couldn't understand why Salesforce.com would not take a meeting with Involver because we were in the same space with similar technology and could be acquired for significantly less than the valuation associated with Buddy Media.

I reached out to Byron Deeter and requested help with an introduction to the corporate development team at Salesforce.com.

He had heard that Salesforce.com had been focused on the integration of Radian6 into their company for the past few months and were not aggressively pursuing other acquisitions. Byron agreed it was a good time for a meeting, and he contacted Ryan Aytay who was with the corporate development team at Salesforce.com.

Byron learned that Salesforce.com was about to increase its interest in social-media acquisitions, and Ryan expressed interest in meeting the executive team at Involver. He suggested an initial meeting with Marc Benioff, which convinced me that if our first meeting was with their CEO, then they were down the path with acquisition discussions with one of our competitors. I assumed, based on the rumors, that it was Buddy Media and possibly Vitrue as well.

The meeting with Salesforce.com was important for many reasons. The company's vision for the social-media enterprise, and specifically social-media marketing, was aligned with what the founders felt was the future of Involver. But it was clear that Involver would never be able to capitalize on this market opportunity alone. We could triple the size of our company and grow revenues fivefold and still be only a small fraction of the market share of our targeted industry. At this point, partnering with a Salesforce.com or Oracle made far more sense than signing a VC term sheet.

Our customers were asking for a complete end-to-end solution for their social-media marketing requirements. This included visual authoring, publishing, monitoring, analytics, commerce, community management, experience management, and ad management. We just couldn't compete as a standalone company when going against a robust social-media solution vision that could only be built by industry leaders such as Oracle or Salesforce.com.

Our employees were very important to me, and Salesforce.com would be a great company for them to work for in San Francisco. The company headquarters was just a few blocks away, and their reputation for quality of work life was second to none in our industry. Our young employees took pride in working in the city of San Francisco, and many were not interested in relocating anywhere else in the valley. San Francisco had become the epicenter for social-media skills in

Silicon Valley with the majority of successful social-media companies located in the city. Salesforce.com would be a great home for the employees of Involver.

We prepped for the meeting just like we did for Oracle. Despite being dramatically smaller in size, we felt we had a similar culture to Salesforce.com. We believed that Marc Benioff would relate to some of the personal stories of Involver and the founders. We also felt strongly that we had the technology and talent to contribute to Marc's commitment to addressing the needs of the social-media enterprise. The talent acquisition was key because our employees had the social DNA that both Oracle and Salesforce.com wanted to acquire. We assumed Marc knew that Oracle would be making an investment in this space very soon, and he was probably motivated to make the first move.

The talent acquisition was important but so was our technology. There are two core areas where Involver fits—engagement across public social networks (primary) and customer social networks (secondary). Salesforce.com already had assets for each of these areas with its acquisition of Radian6 and SiteForce. The key thing would be for the Involver executive team to convince Marc that in public social networks, marketers needed experience management (Involver) in addition to community management (Radian6). Involver's expertise could also be instrumental in helping build out the social road map for SiteForce.

Basic themes for the meeting mapped out by Rahim included the following:

1. We have a great founding and operating team that understands the dynamics of the social-media industry.
2. We believe in his big vision around social-media enterprise and creating a $10 billion–plus social CRM (customer relationship management) company. Social CRM is a philosophy and a business strategy supported by a technology platform, business rules, workflow, processes, and social characteristics designed to engage the customer in a collaborative conversation in

order to provide mutually beneficial value in a trusted and transparent business environment.

3. In social-media marketing today, there are two components: community and experiences. (Ads is a third, and we have a way to integrate into that ecosystem.)

4. Social-media experiences are complex to provide, and Involver makes experiences easy (product demo and narrative) and has better technology and vision than the competition.

5. Involver can make the social-media marketing cloud more complete, both today and in the future.

The much-anticipated meeting with Marc Benioff, CEO of Salesforce.com, occurred on April 16 at the company's headquarters in downtown San Francisco. We felt extremely prepared for our presentation. The meeting was to start at five o'clock that evening but was delayed by Marc due to some scheduling conflicts. Rahim, Noah, and I sat in a conference room waiting patiently for more than an hour and a half with members of the corporate development team from Salesforce.com.

While waiting, we asked them how we should best facilitate the discussion with their CEO. Their corporate development team simply said that Marc would determine the agenda and content he wished to discuss and that we would need to follow his lead. I was also concerned about how much time we would have with Marc, because it was getting late into the evening. We were told that he had a dinner appointment with a financial analyst at seven o'clock, but he would give us adequate time because he felt the meeting with Involver was important.

We arrived at his office at six thirty, and it was everything we expected. *Star Wars* memorabilia, surfboards, and numerous pictures of Marc with President Obama highlighted his office. Memories from his career at Saleforce.com were present in every corner of his office. He gave the impression that he was extremely proud of what he had accomplished in his career but also did not take himself too seriously and had a keen sense of humor. Despite an intimidating height of approximately six five, he was warm and receptive to our visit. I mentioned that we were sensitive to his time constraints and asked how much time we would have that evening to tell the Involver story. He told us not to worry about the time and requested we start to tell the story of Involver.

My opening comments thanked him for his time and his interest in Involver. I then shared a brief history of Involver and also mentioned the level of interest Involver had received from other companies. I communicated that we were in the corporate development process with a number of firms, including a large competitor of Salesforce. com. We expected the process to be completed within two to three weeks. I also stated that with one company (I did not mention Oracle by name), we'd had approximately one dozen meetings, including a five-hour architectural review.

My comments did not faze him. He looked me in the eyes with a steely glare and said emphatically, "Don, you should know everybody is talking to everybody. Whatever company you are referring to, I can guarantee they are also talking to your competitors."

That being said, both the founders and I felt the acquisition of Involver would be a perfect fit for Salesforce.com. Specifically, the more we learned about Salesforce.com and Marc's vision of the social-media enterprise, the more compelling the prospect of a partnership became. We saw the following mutual benefits:

- We had a shared vision for the social-media enterprise.
- We had complementary technology and solutions that filled gaps in Salesforce.com's solution portfolio that we felt would be critical to leveraging the company's existing social-media investments.
- Both companies had a similar operational culture that we would explain in more detail during our presentation.

I then proposed the following agenda:

- history of the company/founder overview

- company overview (investor presentation style)
- demo of the product
- competitive landscape and why we are different
- from there, it would go to informal Q&A

Marc had a reputation in Silicon Valley of being a very employee-centric CEO in that Salesforce.com was annually recognized as one of the top one hundred companies to work for in *Fortune Magazine.* In a recent *Fortune Magazine* issue, a story was referenced on how he personally helped one of his employees who was dealing with a life-threatening illness. This is the same compassion that was exemplified by Rahim when he started Involver to help a person who was suffering from leukemia and required a bone-marrow transplant. We started our presentation with this story to show the similar cultures of the two companies.

Throughout the meeting, Marc demonstrated his brilliance. He liked our stories but wanted to jump right to the product demo. He immediately saw the advantage of a company delivering a visual authoring tool (VSML) on a scalable platform (SML). But he also commented that the product was too new to determine its value, and we had not developed enough capability yet. He compared us to one of our competitors, Wildfire, who had developed more than one hundred social templates. It was a huge apple-to-orange comparison, but we understood his point.

He also wanted to see the actual code. This was surprising because it was not something we anticipated from a CEO of a multibillion-dollar company. But Marc was a unique executive, and we turned that request to Noah who did an excellent job of showing our code and the advantages of the SML platform.

He also was very candid about how much he knew our space and strongly implied that all major enterprise software companies were not only talking to Involver but also to our competition. He said that if his competition (not mentioning by name Oracle, Adobe, SAP, or IBM) were trying to convince Involver that discussions regarding acquisition were exclusive to us, then we were being misled. Everybody was shopping in this space. Most enterprise software companies were assessing what their social-media strategies would be; inquiries into companies like Involver was just "tire kicking" until their strategies were formulated.

At the end of the meeting, he looked to his corporate development executives for their assessment of the content presented by Involver.

"Well," Marc said to his team. "What do you think about what you heard from Involver?"

I was somewhat surprised that he asked his team while we were still in the room, but I was extremely interested in their answers to his question. Their responses were not overwhelmingly positive or negative, and we could not determine what level of interest they had with Involver. They just said that they were overall impressed and that we would be hearing from them soon. They gave us encouragement but definitely no buying signs. The session ended with Marc requesting his team stay to debrief on the meeting and for the Involver team to depart into the night.

Rahim, Noah, and I left the meeting in the dark of San Francisco not knowing if we had been successful in positioning Involver as a good acquisition candidate for Salesforce.com. We left the meeting slightly after eight o'clock, a credit to Marc that he was sincerely interested in learning more about Involver. We were frustrated that we were unable to gain a commitment from the participating Salesforce.com executives for a follow-up meeting.

That evening I could not sleep. Even though I felt extremely prepared for the meeting, I kept thinking of all the things I wish I had said to Marc Benioff during our time at Salesforce.com.

Salesforce.com, Stage Two:

THE NEXT MORNING I called the corporate development executives at Salesforce.com to gain their assessment of the success of the meeting. I was pleased to hear they wanted to have a very detailed day with key members of the Involver team to understand all aspects of our business. This was similar to the five-hour architectural review session held with Oracle, and we felt it was a very good sign. The date was set for April 27.

But the call was also an opportunity to determine what areas of concern existed for Salesforce.com in regards to a potential acquisition with Involver. There were seven areas of concern expressed to me by the company's corporate development team. With the help of Noah and Rahim, I responded to these seven concerns via both e-mail and a personal conversation with the corporate development executives. I scripted my responses to their concerns so that I could address each issue clearly and concisely. The concerns were as follows:

1. **Lack of social analytics.** I understood that social analytics was a powerful tool for uncovering customer sentiment dispersed across countless online sources. (A good example was when we chose to partner with business-intelligent firms that specialized in this area as opposed to building it ourselves.) We focused on the collection of the data and not building the analytical tools ourselves. Our largest customers had also specifically asked that we specialize in this collection and simply make the data available via API for them to consume in the BI tool of choice. The visualization element of analytics was lacking in our current offering, but we were solving this through a partnership with a BI tool vendor. We also saw this as an advantage with Salesforce. com as we could easily plug our data into the visualization mechanisms in R6.

2. **Lack of multi-language support.** We were unsure of their concern here but thought perhaps we didn't demo this well enough. Involver had some of the best multi-language support in the industry. All of our tools had internationalized interfaces, and we had done some translations of it already (largely to Japanese). In fact, our automated UI testing was all built on top of our internationalization work, so we knew it was comprehensive.

3. **Too few widgets—harder pitch for our sales team without a large widget portfolio.** (A software widget is a relatively simple and easy-to-use software application or component made for one or more different software platforms. With Involver, this was a simple drag-and-drop functional capability such as a YouTube video.) We had launched twenty-one widgets in six weeks and were preparing to launch two more complex widgets. That was with only two developers working exclusively on widgets. Looking at our development rate, it was clear that we would surpass all of our competitors in widget counts in 2012, even without adding additional resources to the effort. More important was that because of the nesting and compassable nature of our widgets, it was not an apples-to-apples comparison. An example is that a sign-up form that then gives the user a success message, a sign-up form that then lets the user send a virtual gift to her friend, and a sign-up form that then lets a user print a coupon would be three different widgets in our competitors systems. In ours, it was one sign-up widget made up of three other widgets (text, gifts, and coupon). If you wanted to gate the same three widgets on verifying the user's age, that would be with the addition of one age-gate widget in our system, whereas it would be another three completely separate widgets for our competitors. Thus, we could match their functionality with fewer widgets needed. A final note was that our win rates on this product demonstrated that the widget set is sufficient to win more deals than we lost on VSML.

4. **Social channel coverage.** We were not sure we understood their concern because we had most of the core social-media landscape covered with the exception of LinkedIn (and could integrate if necessary).

5. **Burning more cash than expected.** Our cost base was capital efficient. We were burning approximately $300,000 per month (mainly due to recent sales and G&A investments) and were tracking for profitability by the end of the year.

6. **Bridge loans were a concern.** We were very close to finalizing our M&A options and did not want to take a round to further dilute our stock position. Our investors had deep pockets and were very supportive of the company. If we didn't find a deal that was acceptable, we would sign a VC term sheet.

7. **Overlapping technology.** Indeed, we did have some overlap in technology. However, that was demonstrative of us both having similar market visions. SML and VSML are incredibly solid products with a large developer community and adoption. Radian6 and Conversation Suite did have overlap, but I believed that our UX was very impressive and customer feedback validated that, and it (or portions of it) could be married to the Radian6 infrastructure to improve that product. In both places, the complementary teams would greatly accelerate the road maps and industry adoption for all teams.

On April 27, we held a full-day meeting at Salesforce.com to conduct a detailed assessment of Involver and our technology. In attendance from Salesforce.com were not only the company's technical team but also the technical leadership from Radian6. Because this meeting was scheduled on a Friday, it was quite an imposition to have the Radian6 technical team attend meeting in person. This required an overnight stay because their headquarters was located in Canada. We took this as a positive sign that they were sincerely interested in our company.

The day went as expected. We broke into two groups. Noah and his technical team went through our technology in detail with the attending CTOs of Salesforce.com. Rahim and I reviewed the company's strategy and financials with members of the corporate development team.

As I was presenting the company financials, I knew the fact that we had bridge loans to ensure our financial viability. I presented the content and was open about our cash position as well as our dependency from outside parties for loans. I tried to downplay this point, but the corporate development team from Salesforce.com would not let me move on to other topics without a more detailed explanation of why we were in this cash position.

I responded as follows: "Please understand that we have stopped looking for funding to explore the M&A alternative. Do not conclude that because we took this path that it means we could not secure investment funding. That is a wrong assumption for your company to make about Involver. As we anticipate the consolidation of the industry, Involver was going to be acquisition targets. Our efforts are to be proactive with this process and work with potential suitors that make the most sense for Involver. To be specific, partners like Salesforce.com!" As I spoke, I wasn't sure he was buying my logic.

By the look on his face, he wasn't buying in to my statement. There are not many ways to spin the fact that you needed short-term financing to stay in business. We could not hide the fact that we were short on cash and required short-term bridge loans to stay in business. I could sense this was a growing concern.

I was hoping that our efforts with Oracle and Salesforce.com would be successful enough to stimulate a bidding war for Involver. This might have been my personal fantasy, but I attempted to leave the impression with both Oracle and Salesforce.com that we had interest from other parties and that it would be in their best interest to present a term sheet sooner rather than later.

The cold reality was that we needed a term sheet sooner rather than later because our cash position continued to be a concern, and time was not on our side. Potential acquirers did not always match our sense of urgency, and because we did not have a competitive term sheet, there was no compelling reason for any party to act quickly on our behalf.

CHAPTER NINE

Term Sheet

TIME WENT ON, AND as we entered the month of May, we still had no term sheet for acquisition and only had approximately four weeks of cash remaining on our books. What was most concerning was that we had been expecting a term sheet from Oracle based on our conversations over the past few weeks. We had heard that it was in the hands of the company's corporate development group, but there appeared no movement. I reached out to my contacts at Oracle, and they informed me that Larry Ellison and his senior leadership team were too preoccupied with the lawsuit with Google to focus on our term sheet at that time.

Oracle and Google were engaged in a legal dispute related to Oracle's copyright and patent claims on Google's Android operating system. Eventually, in May 2012, the jury in this case found that Google had not infringed on Oracle's patents, and the trial judge ruled that the structure of the Java APIs used by Google was not copyrightable. The parties agreed to zero dollars in statutory damages for a small amount of copied code.

This did not make sense, because it would be a surprise that Larry Ellison would be involved with an acquisition of this size. My contacts at Oracle also implied that we were not the only acquisition in the queue, and our term sheet may not be the top priority. I could understand this, but did it mean that the company was in the process of acquiring one of our competitors? Something was up, and I had no idea what the future held in regards to our relationship with Oracle.

A Difficult Board Meeting:

WE HELD A BOARD meeting on May 8 to discuss the status of our acquisition efforts. We had to be prepared to share with the board our best-case (term sheet) and worst-case (shut down costs associated with closing Involver) scenarios. This meeting was of critical importance. We planned on covering some very tactical actions associated with our M&A process, as well as contingency plans if things did not go as planned. Because of these unique circumstances, the board meeting would be very different from ones of the past.

We had prepared content to discuss first-quarter attainment and key accomplishments. Despite the many distractions that had plagued this company over the past 120, days including lack of funding and rumors among the employee base about our future, we made it clear to the board that we still had accomplished a great deal, including

- Q1 Bookings of $2 million, including exciting new logos (such as Pepsi and Coke);
- a Super Bowl Ad Meter Campaign and Case Study with Facebook;
- one million pages powered by Involver;
- recalibration of the sales organization and five new sales resources;
- new product positioning and pricing;
- a new website launch; and
- management to maintain the integrity of the business.

And most importantly, our engineering team had been successful in delivering key new products to the market, including

- VSML launch and sales training;

- Conversation Suite launch and sales training; and
- Optimization API launches with strategic partners Marin and Unified.

I told the board, "Although we at Involver are very proud of these accomplishments, we had to face reality of our business, and that is that we have only thirty days of cash remaining. Almost every person on the Involver executive team has made personal sacrifices to preserve cash (including personal loans and reduced compensation), but this is a reality we must address immediately."

The board agreed.

The board was not aware of all the commitments we had made, so it was time to let them know our level of sacrifice.

I continued. "Rahim, Noah, and I reduced our salaries by 50 percent to preserve cash over the past few months. We also traded cash for stock incentive on our bonus plans. We were all personally committed to the success of Involver with our hearts, minds, and wallets. This was the epitome of our personal sacrifice. It is important that the board is aware of this point." I spoke firmly.

The board appreciated this commitment.

I asked the board's permission to not discuss traditional board content, such as the financial performance over the first few months of the year. I wanted to focus on the only relevant issues that were on all our minds and discuss only the following topics:

- M&A status and action plan and associated timeline
- cash balance and challenges
- shutdown costs and actions and associated timeline

Everyone was in agreement that we needed focus on the task at hand, and that was obtaining a term sheet as quickly as possible. While Oracle and Salesforce.com were still our best options, other smaller companies had shown interest. We decided to continue to aggressively pursue the former and sent out bid process letters to any potential buyer with a deadline to submit a response by May 21.

I now had to bring up the eight-hundred-pound gorilla in the room. This topic was not one the Involver team wanted to discuss, but the board would force the conversation if we did not bring it up. What would be required to shut down the business if a term sheet was not reached?

I told the board that if we were unsuccessful with the pending M&A process, then we would embark on shutting down the majority of the company.

"We have to face facts that shutting down a significant portion of the company is a real possibility, and these shut down costs will not be insignificant to the board of directors who would have to incur the majority of this expense. We have estimated this expense to be approximately $1.8 million, made up of salaries (one paycheck), severance PTO costs (paid time off), commission bonuses, contractor pay, accounts payable, and miscellaneous tax fees and other contingencies," I stated, knowing that my message was not well received.

The mood in the room changed dramatically, and the board was not pleased with this information. They invested in Involver to make money, not lose their investments and then pay shutdown costs.

None of the Involver executive team had been forced to shut down a business before, so we were all very inexperienced in this area. What this meant was that if we did not receive a term sheet in approximately two weeks, then we would execute a sale for company assets and dramatically cut all expenses except for the engineering resources needed to maintain our products in the market. This was a reality that we all we had to acknowledge and be ready to execute within the next two weeks.

The majority of the discussion at the board meeting revolved around why we had not received a term sheet despite interest from outside parties. The board was critical (and rightfully so) about the claims of valuation expectation by the founders and me. We were closest to the company and felt our valuation expectations were higher than what our board was projecting.

To be exact, when asked during both the funding and acquisition road shows for valuation expectations, we never directly answered their questions. We stated we would let the process determine valuation but took the opportunity to share the success we had achieved since our last funding round. This included the following information: In the past eighteen months we had doubled revenues and had refreshed our entire product line. We also had 1 million accounts with an active Facebook fan page powered by Involver.

Based on these milestones, we felt we had made significant progress since our last valuation and believed the company was far more valuable than it had been previously.

The board felt this was a mistake. We could be pricing ourselves out of the market. We needed to stop our focus on securing an attractive valuation and become relentless in our efforts to just get a term sheet. The board was perfectly clear that our immediate goal was to get a term sheet from any party. From there, we could leverage a short window of opportunity to open the process up for bid and determine if there was any other interest from another potential company. The perfect scenario would be to facilitate a bidding war with multiple parties to increase the sale price. The first step was to get that first term sheet in the door.

Fishing:

IMMEDIATELY AFTER THE BOARD meeting, I reached out to talk to Kumar at Oracle. I really pressed him for answers. I first asked if there was anything holding up a term sheet other than price. He stated that he did not think that price was an issue, but that was up to corporate development. He did say that there was an internal reason for the holdup at Oracle for a term sheet and that he could not elaborate with me due to its sensitive nature. His bottom line was that it was unlikely that Oracle could react in submitting a term sheet in the time frame we had put forward until this internal issue had been addressed.

Kumar was a true professional and would not share confidential information with me at any time, and I would never ask a personal friend to be put in that position. I assumed that this was probably reorganization where the executive sponsor endorsing the Involver acquisition would not own the business plan in the immediate future. The reason I believed this was that he kept saying it was an internal issue and not related to any outside acquisitions or due diligence. I asked for his advice on this matter, and he said our only path would be to cut a deal with the corporate development team at Oracle. No advice was given or received on valuation. Again, Kumar's advice made sense, and I did not compromise our friendship by requesting any information that could be viewed as confidential.

I met with Rahim and Noah after the call and discussed what our next steps should be. Noah had made a very positive connection with Thomas Kurian during one of our meetings a few weeks back. They shared the same vision and passion to capture market share with a joint solution offering. I suggested to Noah that he send Thomas an e-mail requesting a brief conversation. We felt we had nothing to lose.

In his May 8 e-mail, Noah expressed deep conviction to Thomas Kurian and his desire for Involver to be a part of the solution portfolio being built by Oracle. He stressed that he had dedicated more than five years building a business that he was extremely passionate about but would never achieve its true potential unless it was combined with a company like Oracle who brought the technology and resources necessary to capitalize on the vast market opportunity in front of us. He mentioned that we had met with many companies, but the vision interlock between Oracle and Involver had been the most enticing.

Noah also mentioned how impressed he had been that Thomas had read some of the developer documentation. He felt he'd really done his homework on Involver. Together, our two companies were better positioned to succeed in the ever-changing social-media marketing industry. He closed by stating our confusion regarding why discussions had slowed down in regards to our proposed partnership.

He mentioned the board meeting and discussions on other acquisition options but again stressed his desire to work with Oracle. The e-mail was a very well-written and powerful message to Oracle.

It must have made an impact on Thomas, because he called Noah the very next day. Thomas stated his continued interest in Involver and plans to accelerate the process. Thomas was meeting with Larry Ellison that afternoon. These actions led us to believe there was a chance of a term sheet within the next few days.

On May 9 we finally received word that Larry Ellison had approved the term sheet for the acquisition of Involver. We received it the same day. Oracle was very good at this process, and we had a very short period of time to approve the term sheet and start the M&A due diligence process. We held a board conference call on Sunday night, May 13, and the term sheet was unanimously approved. I signed it that evening and sent it to our investment banker to share with Oracle.

A Devastating Rumor:

ORACLE HAD THE EARNED reputation of being one of the best companies in the technology sector for its professional merger-and-acquisition methodology. Regardless of the size of the company, it was well known that Oracle had a very detailed process that all companies went through when being acquired. It started with a list of requested content—to say it was extensive would be an understatement. We had to provide literally hundreds of requested documents that addressed the detailed status of each business function within Involver. All business functions were exposed to this scrutiny. No line of business within Involver was left out of this due diligence process.

Although I was impressed with the detail of their due diligence, it was quite a task for the Involver team to address all these documentation requirements. At this point, only a small number of Involver executives were aware of the term sheet from Oracle, and these individuals worked to get the information to Oracle as quickly as possible. Our feeling was that the sooner the due diligence was completed, the faster the transaction and change of control would be completed. We felt we had approximately 85 percent to 90 percent of the requests completed within seventy-two hours. We made this a top priority, and we had momentum on our side.

We had a team of trusted executives work diligently both days and evenings to get this content to Oracle with the hope that we could accelerate the M&A process before running out of cash. Oracle did not always share the same sense of urgency.

Despite our committed focus to the M&A process at Oracle, we started hearing rumors that Oracle had agreed to buy Vitrue, one of our top competitors. This was extremely concerning. Why would they need both of us? Although Vitrue was bigger than Involver, we, at times, beat the company in head-to-head sales engagements and even displaced a few of its customers. Our feeling was that with Oracle's sales and marketing capability, our technology could be proliferated throughout the industry. I guess we were a little naïve on Vitrue and their strengths compared to Involver. If this rumor were true, then our feeling was that the term sheet we received from Oracle could possibly not be honored. This would be devastating to our company and employees.

I immediately called Kumar and questioned him on the rumor of an Oracle acquisition of Vitrue.

"Kumar," I said with a desperate tone, "I do not want to put our personal friendship or professional relationship at risk, but I need to ask you a very important question. I know it will be very difficult for you to answer, but I need to ask the question. I am hearing rumors that Oracle is buying our competitor Vitrue. This would be devastating news to Involver. Is it true?"

I heard nothing but silence on the end of the line. I knew the answer before a word was spoken by Kumar.

"You know I can't answer that question even if it is true. What are you worried about?" he asked.

I replied, "Is Oracle using a term sheet with Involver as a negotiation ploy with Virtue?"

"Let me answer your concerns the only way I can," Kumar responded. "I will not preannounce any M&A activity of Oracle to anybody, not even a good friend. You know that already. But I will say this. Oracle takes its M&A process very seriously. We are very respected in the industry in this regard. We would never issue a term sheet without plans to honor it. We have a long history of acquiring companies after a term sheet is issued, and the number of transactions that don't happen for whatever reason is extremely, extremely small."

I knew he could not say anything to me, but in a panic move, I felt I had nothing to lose. I understood and apologized for putting him in that position with my questions. I was extremely concerned that we were being used only as leverage with Oracle's negotiations and that the company's interest in us was to take us off the market for a period of time so that Salesforce.com could not make an acquisition bid. He stated we had nothing to worry about in that regard.

Confusion and Chaos:

THE FOLLOWING WEEK (MAY 23, 2012) Oracle issued a press release announcing that it has entered an agreement to acquire Virtue, a major competitor to Involver. It went on to state that the transaction was expected to close in the summer of 2012. The press release went on to share the joint opportunity that combining both companies could recognize with the proliferation of social media and how it had changed the way organizations and consumers interact. Together, Oracle and Virtue announced their plans to unify the social experience across customer interactions, resulting in meaningful customer engagements with consistent brand experiences across all channels and media. This also included their goal of improving the return on investment for social-media sales and marketing campaigns as well as enhancing customer service through real-time responsiveness and high-touch engagements.

The deal was estimated in the $300 million range. As you can imagine, this caused confusion and concern among all employees at

Involver. Despite our best attempts to keep our acquisition activity a secret, rumors were prevalent that Oracle and Salesforce.com would be the most likely suitors for Involver. This was why many of our employees stayed with Involver. Now that Oracle had announced its intentions with Vitrue, most of our employees wondered what, if any, conclusions could be drawn by this announcement in regards to Involver's immediate future.

Many of our valued employees came up to my desk and simply asked the question. "Did you hear the news of the acquisition of Vitrue by Oracle? What do you make of it, and what does it mean to Involver?"

That was not an easy question to answer. All I could say was that it was good for the industry and good for Involver. The consolidation of our industry had begun, and there was one less company we needed to compete with because any integration efforts by a company the size of Oracle could open opportunities for Involver.

Was I worried? Hell yes. Did I show it? Not to our employees. But this had become a distraction that was very disruptive as we strived to keep an environment of business as usual in the company. We immediately scheduled an all-hands meeting where I continued to reinforce the prediction that the industry consolidation would occur and that no surprise should come from this announcement of Oracle acquiring Vitrue.

Rahim, who was highly respected by the company in regards to his understanding of the social-media industry dynamics sent out an e-mail to the employee population in an attempt to bring some sort of normalcy to the operations at Involver. In this e-mail, he acknowledged Oracle's acquisition of Vitrue and positioned it accordingly as the expected consolidation of the enterprise marketing space. This acquisition was actually very good news for Involver, our customers, and everyone in the domain. This announcement was also very good for Involver's strategic options. He also communicated another very important point in his e-mail in that our existing partnership discussions had also accelerated. This announcement legitimized the fact that social-media marketing was a true enterprise software class that had attracted the attention of the most powerful entities in the industry.

This e-mail was the right message. All employees needed to be reassured that this was actually good news for Involver and that our industry sector continued to be the focus of the major forces in the high-tech industry. This validated that Involver was in the right place at the right time.

Just when we thought that nothing could be more distracting than the Oracle announcement with Vitrue, Salesforce.com made its leap into the social-media marketing world with a press release eleven days later on June 4, announcing the acquisition of Buddy Media for approximately $689 million payable in cash and Salesforce.com equity. The transaction was expected to close during Salesforce.com's fiscal third quarter ending October 31, 2012.

Approximately $1 billion had been spent in eleven days on social-media marketing companies in our space!

If our employee base was confused before this news, then the Salesforce.com announcement could create panic. We needed to get the entire company assembled and address the announcements that had occurred over the past two weeks and, most importantly, what it meant to the employees of Involver. With both Oracle and Salesforce.com playing their cards, the future of a company like Involver was in question to our employees. What our employees did not know was that we had a term sheet from Oracle. We could not share any information regarding this fact with employees until the merger agreement was signed. But we had to reassure the company that our future was fine. This would not be easy.

The employees' concerns were understandable and justified. Oracle, with its published commitment to social CRM leadership, was gaining respect in the industry for its investments not only in social media but cloud computing as well. Salesforce.com, whose focus on the social-media enterprise was well documented, was positioning Oracle for a market-share battle. Our employees probably felt that these two high-tech giants would become the winners in the social-media marketing industry. Where would that leave Involver?

We again gathered the employee base for an all-hands discussion. We had some very key messages to deliver. Rahim and I would deliver the meeting content.

My role was to kick off the meeting by acknowledging the latest announcements and the rumors running rampant throughout Involver regarding our future. I also let employees know that we were involved with very strategic discussions, and any dialog on these developments would require a high level of discretion. We wanted to share our confidence in our future but also protect our interest in the confidential discussions with Oracle and the integrity of Involver.

Rahim then went into more detail, explaining that we had been in conversations with several potential partners in recent weeks, and these discussions have led to one partner with especially strong interest in the company. There was mutual interest from both parties, and we were equally excited about this proposed partnership. He mentioned that at the time we couldn't give specific information on any specific partner or timing of a potential announcement. What we could tell them was that the interested company saw social media as a strategic part of its future offering and had the resources to ensure our mutual success in capitalizing on the large opportunity in our industry.

I closed the meeting by asking all employees to focus on their current roles and responsibilities at Involver and not to get distracted by industry rumors. I also stated that I would do something very different in this all-hands session. I usually closed meetings by providing a forum for the employees to ask me any questions regarding Involver. At every all-hands meeting I wanted any employee to ask me any question regarding the company, its strategy, and its future. But this time I told the team that we had shared all we could share regarding potential partnership discussions with an interested party. I really couldn't answer any further questions. This felt strange to me and was probably somewhat surprising to the employees, but I felt strongly that it was the right thing to do. I did not want to address a line of questioning that would take me where I did not want to go.

The Facebook IPO:

THE SOCIAL-MEDIA INDUSTRY WAS on fire, and things were going to get more interesting very soon. At about this same time, Facebook launched its IPO. Facebook's trading debut was on May 18, and it was a great disappointment. The stock opened initially very strong at $42.05, up 11 percent from its offer price ($38). At one point, it even jumped as high as 18 percent and hit $45. But then things did not go in Facebook's favor. The rally lost momentum throughout the day. After much volatility, the stock closed at a disappointing $38.23, up 23 cents, or 0.6 percent.

What investors and analysts had predicted never came true. Trading volume set a record for the most ever shares traded (more than 573 million shares changed hands) for a US stock the day of its IPO. The stock continued its decline over the next few weeks. While investor enthusiasm was high for the company's shares before the IPO, leading bankers on the deal decided to increase the stock price and number of shares to be offered ahead of the IPO date. NASDAQ was also to be blamed for the poor support of the high trading volumes. Before and after the IPO, Facebook faced scrutiny in regards to the $100 billion valuation being placed on the social network, while industry analyst continued questioning the company's revenue and earnings growth projections.

Implications for the social-media marketing industry were significant. Facebook's disappointing public trading debut could have a negative impact on everything from IPO valuations to venture capital funding for social-media companies in the months ahead. This meant that social start-ups starving for additional funding would have even a more difficult time raising money.

Facebook generated 85 percent of its $3.7 billion in 2011 revenues from global online ad sales. Many companies initially utilized Facebook to promote their brands while paying little or nothing for this service. As Facebook looked for more ways to monetize their ad sales, more brands were concerned if additional investments would actually yield greater product sales. Brands were demanding answers from Facebook. If a company committed additional investments with Facebook in online ad spending, what would be the return on that investment? How could an investment in Facebook be quantified to justify future expenditures based on future generated business value?

At the time, Facebook had no real answer to this question. Quarterly ad revenue growth was declining at this time, and Facebook had an emerging credibility problem. Just because a user "liked" a page, that did not necessarily lead to a purchase. The confusion over the benefits of social-media marketing continued to be debated by industry analysts. Valuations of social-media start-ups would be scrutinized more than ever after Facebook failed to meet industry expectations with its IPO.

The IPO market was shaken, and the valuations of social-media start-ups were diminishing under greater scrutiny from potential investors. In June, a new Reuters poll reported that 34 percent of Facebook users were spending less time on the site than they had six months earlier, while only 20 percent were spending more time on the site. Meanwhile, the poll also found that 80 percent of Facebook users had never bought a product or service as a result of advertising or comments on the site. The poll magnified investors' worries about Facebook's revenue-producing capabilities. The stock was down 29 percent since its initial public offering, reducing its market value by $30 billion to roughly $74 billion.

Despite the disappointing Facebook IPO, Salesforce.com and Oracle were still making strong statements to the market that social media was going to be very strategic for both companies. Salesforce. com not only purchased Buddy Media but had also acquired Radian6 (social-media monitoring) a year earlier, strengthening the company's social-media position dramatically. Oracle not only acquired Vitrue but also acquired Collective Intellect, a social-media intelligence company within the same month. This was becoming a race to deliver the best end-to-end marketing application stack for social-media CRM.

It was clear that these companies were now aggressively acquiring the social-media DNA and talent they didn't already have. This talent acquisition would be instrumental to productize the various applications into an integrated solution portfolio.

Despite the dynamics occurring in the market, the founders and I felt that Oracle's acquisition of both Vitrue and Involver was a very powerful statement on the importance of social-media technologies and associated talent to the company. We had the term sheet in hand, and if we could accelerate the timing of the acquisition or company change of control, then the worries over our cash balance would no longer be an issue.

CHAPTER TEN

Due Diligence

DESPITE BEING EXTREMELY RESPONSIVE to the numerous requests for information, Oracle was very firm in its timeline for completion of the due diligence. The company's approach was very methodical. They didn't cut corners, and we were told that efforts to accelerate the process would probably not be successful. Because cash was an issue, we were growing more and more frustrated by our inability to move up the signing date. Regardless if you were a $2 million company or a $2 billion company, you would go through the same process and timetable. Negotiations and due diligence might take longer, but a reduced timetable was unrealistic according to Oracle.

I kept thinking about Facebook's April 12, 2012, acquisition of Instagram (free photo-sharing application) and how a $1 billion acquisition of cash and stock was done within twenty-four hours.

There is a fundamental difference between companies that are sold and companies that are bought. We were definitely for sale, and that took a great deal of leverage away from our ability to negotiate terms in our favor. Early on in my tenure at Involver, I received an e-mail from a banker soliciting my interest in acquiring a company that was "complementary" to Involver. I felt the company's business was nothing close to Involver and felt sorry for the CEO who I felt was conducting a fire sale for his company.

We divided the work up among the executive team on what responsibilities we would be accountable for during the due diligence process. Rahim took ownership in a number of areas, including the management contracts of key employees. From Oracle's perspective, these were to be mostly engineers and developers. Noah worked on the technology platform and the transition of the developers at Involver.

I took on sales and marketing, as well as representing Rahim and Noah to Oracle. This was important to me, because I had witnessed firsthand the sacrifices these two individuals had made to turn Involver into a success. I made it clear to the senior leadership at Oracle that these two executives were the first employees they should secure at their company. This meant a role and responsibility that leveraged their expertise and compensation commensurate with their value. I made it clear that these were the two most underpaid executives in social media.

Creditors were calling me directly. Rahim, Noah, and I had a corporate card that was now being denied. I had never experienced this before in my career, but I'd also never been a part of a bootstrapped start-up.

Years ago I had a very good friend who became a CEO early in his career after he'd left IBM. I did not know much about his company, but I felt it was great for him to be a CEO at such a young age. He had a great career at IBM and had very strong leadership qualities. I called him to catch up because it had been more than a year since he'd became a CEO and I wanted to know his experience. I remember a timid voice answering the phone that did not announce his name. When he knew it was his old friend, he was pleased that it wasn't a creditor. I thought that was very funny, and then I realized I was the only one laughing. He said creditors were calling day and night, both at work and at home. My only thought was that his days at IBM had not prepared him for going bankrupt. My training hadn't prepared me either.

I did not have it that bad, but I could relate to his experience. This was not fun. What was worst was when my employees (some of which I'd personally hired) were asking why their expenses were not being paid.

Employees would approach me and say something like, "I received my base pay but not my commission. Should I be worried?" Or, "I still have not received my expense reimbursement. What is going on?"

I would reply, "I am sure it is a minor mistake. Let me look into it for you. I am sure it can be easily remedied."

Now, I was convinced that everyone would be paid accurately. It just was dependent on the timing of our cash collectibles. I did not want people to know that their expense payments were tied to our cash balance each month. I would act surprised and make it a priority payment to keep the noise down.

These conversations were very difficult.–This was yet another motivation to get this acquisition done as soon as possible.

Disappointing News and a Silver Lining:

JUST BEFORE WE RECEIVED the term sheet from Oracle, we received news that was extremely disappointing.

On April 30, I was at my desk reading the morning e-mails when I received a troubling message from our largest partner that resold our technology within its solution portfolio. The e-mail announced that the company was developing its own version of our products and would not be reselling anything from Involver effective immediately. The e-mail went on to say:

> We've had an innovative and mutually beneficial partnership to date, and we appreciate all that your team has been able to put into the relationship. Although we have had some bumps and bruises, as well as many wins and successes, along the way working with one another, please know that we value the relationship and the decision to move to our internally developed products is primarily a strategic and economic one.

This did not come as a big surprise, as we anticipated this action was going to happen eventually. The timing was the most challenging. Having our most important business partner inform us that they would be migrating their customers off our solution platform would have a significant impact on our financial performance going forward. This partnership generated approximately $250,000 to $300,000 in business every quarter. We were not sure how Oracle would receive this information during its due diligence process.

After months trying to secure a term sheet from Oracle, we would now have to explain why our best business partner was leaving us because it built capability comparable to Involver. What message did this send to Oracle? Why did our best partner no longer value our products or services? Was it that easy to replicate our technology? What was the impact of this decision to Involver's financial position?

Although this was expected, we had to plan for an immediate shortfall in our bookings for the quarter. But what really surprised the executive team at Involver was that this news also had an incredible silver lining.

Rahim had a great relationship with the executive team of this business partner. In discussing the transition of customers away from our company, there had to be a financial settlement for unpaid business that had yet to be recognized by Involver. The business relationship with this partner included a contract term that stated Involver gets paid only when our partner got paid. This meant that we would not recognize revenues for sixty to ninety days after the transaction was typically completed. In other words, we would be receiving approximately $300,000 in accounts receivables (cash) over the next thirty days that we had not anticipated. This money was desperately needed to see us through our acquisition. If we did not receive this capital, then our cash projections would not have made it to our targeted acquisition timeline.

We also received good news that Involver would be dropped from the class-action lawsuit first brought to my attention when I joined in September 2012. Things were looking up for us as our due diligence process continued with Oracle. I could only imagine the headaches this would have caused with our potential acquirer.

Last-Minutes Delays:

OUR TARGET DATE FOR signing was June 26. This was the date that Oracle communicated to us. Throughout the numerous requests for information and data on our business, there were also some key negotiations regarding the legal terms of the agreement. From the legal document, which was more than one hundred pages long, we had issues over three major concerns:

- **Escrow amount and timing:** The amount of money held back and the duration before it was paid to protect Oracle from any claims against Involver.
- **Indemnification (IP and fraud):** Oracle protection from any misrepresentation/inaccuracies with closing statements, breach, or claims by any party.
- **Employment contracts and retention bonuses:** For key employees, what would be their compensation and any bonus for retention? This typically included engineers and developers critical to the technology.

Most contract negotiation of this nature focuses on these issues. We were anticipating that these would be the major discussion points to a contract. Due to confidentiality, the specific details associated with the negotiations can't be shared, but it came as no surprise that both parties were firm in their positioning. Only one had leverage, and that was Oracle. For the most part, we negotiated in good faith and eventually gained agreement on all terms.

Unfortunately for Involver, our target date of June 26 did not result in a signed agreement. More information was being requested by Oracle. After delivering this newly requested content, we heard from Oracle that its "best and final" proposal for the merger agreement would be submitted to Involver on Friday, June 29. It was now time to gain board approval to sign the agreement first thing the following Monday morning. It was also the first time I perceived a sense of urgency from Oracle to get this signed. The Fourth of July holiday was falling on a Wednesday, and our mutual goal was to have this completed before the holiday. Then we would postpone the official announcement until July 9 for a larger market impact.

Over the weekend, I scheduled a call with the Involver board of directors, as well as our attorneys, to approve the transaction. We briefly discussed the terms and the risk we would all assume under the escrow agreement. We unanimously approved the merger agreement terms and gave our lawyers the green light for signature on Monday.

Unfortunately (again) for Involver, there was no signature event on Monday. To say we were frustrated was an understatement.

Late in the day on Monday, Oracle's attorney expressed concern regarding Involver's cash position and our ability to fund the company through closing. Oracle discussed some changes to the merger agreement and actions that Involver would need to take before any signing commitment. What was ironic was that Involver had more than $400,000 in the bank on June 26, but because Oracle delayed the signing date, this now became an issue. We made payroll at the end of June, which depleted the funds in the bank and caused the concern with Oracle. If we had been able to sign on the original date of June 26, then this would not have been an issue.

Oracle and our attorneys scheduled a call for July 3 to discuss this issue of concern. Their position was very clear—we had to fund the cash shortfall via a short-term loan from one of our investors. We had already secured this commitment from Alnoor Shivji, one of our angel investors and board members. Oracle wanted to see proof. So at the end of the day, we contacted our lawyers and created a promissory note and loan agreement for Alnoor to sign. He wanted to add one reasonable request that the loan was subject to the signing of the merger agreement, and no funds would be transferred until all signatures were secured.

This required board approval. We routed for approval to all board members the loan proposal on Independence Day, July 4. All approvals were secured in the morning and sent to our attorneys.

Our goal was to finalize the merger agreement over the July Fourth weekend. This was extremely difficult because many key executives, as well as legal support, were not always available due to the holiday. Our motivation to get this agreement finalized was that Oracle was committed to announce on Monday, July 9, and had senior leadership scheduled to be at Involver's headquarter office at nine o'clock that morning to welcome our employees to their company. This was the perfect compelling event to secure signatures from our board on Sunday night (July 8).

I informed the board that we would be signing Sunday night. In our discussions with Fenwick (our attorney) throughout the day, Oracle had made its position very clear to our lawyers that the merger agreement was best and final, and the ball was in our court to sign it immediately. Oracle had numerous executives showing up at Involver on Monday morning for an announcement meeting. In order to meet this deadline, the agreement had to be finalized and signed no later than Sunday evening.

Some last-minute details for closure were being addressed through the day in anticipation of the signing Sunday evening. We worked until midnight and routed the required signature pages (or at least most of them) to our attorneys for submission to Oracle.

Now, I had nothing against the legal profession but having too many lawyers working a deal is like having too many chefs in a kitchen. Each wants to earn his or her stripes, which will eventually delay any deal process. We had our attorneys, our investors had their attorneys, and Oracle had its attorneys. All three groups were very talented but had very strong opinions on how to structure the acquisition documents. Although it was a laborious process, I was very pleased with the work from our attorneys at Fenwick.

Sunday night we signed the merger agreement. We were ready to announce the next day. Or so we thought!

CHAPTER ELEVEN

Announcement and Close

At the point of announcement, I was both physically and mentally exhausted. The negotiations had taken all weekend, and the stress associated with these discussions had taken a toll on my mind. On the Sunday before announcement day, the Involver executive team and our board of directors were all busy from early morning until late evening with negotiations with our lawyers and our investor's attorneys. When everything was finalized, there was no celebration. I had only a feeling of relief.

As I walked the streets of downtown San Francisco, my mind was focused on the employees of Involver. How would they receive the news of the acquisition? I stopped for a coffee, but instead of rushing to the office as I always did, I sat by myself in the coffee shop as I reflected on the journey that was coming to its finish line. In my heart, I knew many of the employees would benefit from this acquisition from a career perspective. Others viewed themselves as serial entrepreneurs, and the thought of joining Oracle would be horrifying to that population of our employees. I also wondered if Oracle would be fair to our employees. Would Oracle recognize the great talent on the team and put them in prominent positions in the company? What about Rahim and Noah? Would Oracle value their incredible entrepreneurial spirits? I could not help but wonder what the immediate future had to offer everyone associated with Involver. I was soon to find out.

After reaching the office, I learned that one signature did not come in, and the announcement meeting had to be postponed until Tuesday. This was extremely frustrating news to hear. Even though the delay was only twenty-four hours, we were all anxious to let our employees know of our exciting announcement.

Lawyer-to-lawyer discussions continued most of the day on Monday. These negotiations were not with Oracle but our own legal team. We continued our efforts to clarify the risk-mitigation requirements of the contract among investors. We were all tired and somewhat frustrated by this additional work, but it was important and we did not want to let any legal details be unaddressed before announcement. Because we knew Oracle executives were showing up at our offices Tuesday morning, we knew that this compelling event would ensure our internal legal work would be completed by the end of the day. Tuesday could not arrive soon enough.

I also looked forward to the day when I could walk through the office of Involver without having to play games with our employees regarding the rumors of our pending acquisition. I never lied to an employee. I just withheld confidential information that could not be shared. When asked about a rumor of acquisition, I explained that I could not confirm or deny the rumor. But as we approached announcement day, I would add additional details—for example, if the rumors were true, it would be a good thing for Involver and specifically the employee base. I said it with a big smile. I wanted our employees to know I was excited about our immediate future.

The Announcement:

THE LONG-AWAITED ANNOUNCEMENT TO the employees of Involver was finally scheduled for the morning of Tuesday, July 10, 2012. The worst-kept secret was finally confirmed, and the acquisition of Involver by Oracle was to be made public. Over the past two weeks it had become a major distraction to everybody. Our business had suffered, and the employees were growing restless that nothing was being announced.

At 8:55 a.m. PCT on July 10, I sent the following e-mail to all employees:

Dear Involver employees,

We have signed an agreement to be acquired by Oracle, pending standard closing conditions. This acquisition will help us accelerate our reach and continue to develop industry-leading social media development technology and solutions for our customers.

I am certain this news will generate many questions for our customers, our partners, and of course all of you. I am very excited to share with you the details surrounding this announcement and about what it means for our company and employees. Please plan on attending a mandatory 'All-Hands Meeting' today at 10:30am PT to review the strategic rationale, benefits and next steps associated with this planned acquisition. Representatives from Oracle will be on hand to help answer your questions.

We will hold this in person meeting at our San Francisco office and via conference call and GoToMeeting. There will be a question and answer session following the briefing. Please refer to the instructions below for this important meeting.

Best regards,

Don

I forwarded the announcement to the board and expressed my sincere appreciation for their support. I also thanked them for their patience. This was an ordeal like no other, and the board members had been there for us when we needed them the most, especially

Alnoor Shivji who committed the necessary funds at the very end of the process to complete the transaction. I'm not sure where we would be without his commitment to the success of the company sale. I must have told him that ten times.

The employees in San Francisco and our guests from Oracle gathered into our small boardroom. The room could hold fifty people comfortably, and the attendance must have exceeded twice that amount. The city would have definitely fined for a fire hazard, because everybody was shoulder to shoulder. As uncomfortable as people were in the room, they were extremely interested to hear more details of the news.

I kicked it off by getting right to the point of the meeting, which was the announcement of the agreement to be acquired by Oracle. I let everybody know that the acquisition was still subject to some formal approvals and certain other closing conditions but was expected to close within the next few weeks. I then thanked the employees for their continued focus on their day jobs, despite many rumors that had become such a distraction.

I then told the team why I was excited about the acquisition.

"This is truly a great day in the brief history of Involver. I am excited about this announcement for a number of reasons. First, it had become clear (to me and the founders) that we could not capitalize on the enormous business opportunity in our industry alone. There is not a better partner than Oracle. We have a shared vision for what the combined companies can do together in the market. Second, I am also excited for the career prospects at Oracle for the people at Involver. It is a great company that has an incredible future. Our team would be at the forefront of a new direction by Oracle highlighted by their commitment and investments in social and their Public Cloud, which was recently announced in the past few weeks," I stated enthusiastically.

I concluded that I was also very proud that the numerous contributions to the success of Involver, especially during the past year, by our valued employees had made us an attractive partner to Oracle. For that, I was grateful.

It was then time for the employees to hear from the founders. Rahim went first and was passionate about what he and Noah had built at Involver and reminisced about the early days of the company. He stood tall in the front of the conference room, beaming with pride. His smile never left his face. I could only image what he was thinking. I watched as he addressed the company and also felt great pride for both founders.

Rahim thanked the employees for their contributions to this success and noted that the original vision for Involver had been achieved. He displayed excitement but also some emotion that this journey had, in many ways, come to an end. He then shared his perspectives on what could be accomplished with a partner like Oracle. He mentioned that Oracle brought complementary solutions, distribution capability, and research-and-development resources Involver so desperately needed to succeed. It was a very powerful message that was very well received. The company respected Rahim greatly. I could sense everyone's appreciation for the numerous sacrifices the founders made during this amazing journey. It was time for Noah to share in the well-deserved spotlight.

Noah shared his perspective of the acquisition, focusing most of his comments on our current solution portfolio and what could be done to enhance our intellectual property by partnering with Oracle. He expressed sincere interest in being a part of the Oracle vision for social-media and cloud-based technologies. He was impactful in explaining how our combined entity would bring complementary technology that we sincerely felt would be a competitive differentiator in the industry.

I then thanked both founders and asked for the entire company to give them a round of applause for taking a vision five years ago and making this day a reality. This was another milestone in their brilliant careers. In unison, the employees rose to their feet and gave a warm round of applause in appreciation for what the founders had accomplished. The room was small but filled shoulder to shoulder with employees and special guests from Oracle. The small room made the applause deafening. I could see the emotion in the eyes of the founders.

At that time, I wanted to share my thoughts on Oracle. I stood in front of the conference room and stated, "I want everyone to recognize that I know Oracle better than anyone in our company. I am from the enterprise software industry where Oracle today is most dominant in the industry. I have many friends at Oracle, and they love working for the company. They are known in the industry as a fierce competitor. I know this to be true since I have competed with Oracle for many years of my career. They also have outstanding talent across all business functions. I also feel strongly that this is extremely good news to everyone from a career perspective." I made this point with conviction, because I truly believed it was true. I emphasized how our employees would greatly benefit by being a part of this great company.

I also stressed to our employees that this was a very strategic acquisition for Oracle. Involver employees were anxiously waiting to hear directly from the Oracle executives in attendance about how the two companies together would leverage their complementary strengths and, more specifically, what it meant to their careers.

Oracle wanted to strengthen its offering in social media, and we were an extremely good fit because we filled a critical need in the company's public cloud solution portfolio. It was also important for all Involver employees to know that this decision to buy Involver was made with a lot of forethought and deliberation. Oracle felt we could enable a significant competitive advantage for its company. The founders and I truly believed it was the right move for Involver, our communities, and our future.

At that time, I turned the meeting over to Oracle. I have to admit that after the very difficult negotiation process, the comments from their executive team made the entire company feel extremely important to their company.

Abhay Parasnis, senior vice president of Oracle's Public Cloud, provided greater insight to Involver's value to Oracle. To be honest, he could not have done a better job. He explained that although the intellectual property acquired by Oracle was important, our technology would most likely change dramatically over time. That was the nature of our fast-growing industry. What really mattered to Oracle were the people. The employees of Involver were the real assets in this acquisition.

What a great message! The Involver team heard him loud and clear, and if there was any apprehension with the employees before the meeting about joining a large company like Oracle, I felt his words provided encouragement to begin their new journeys with open minds. I talked to many employees after the meeting from our offices in San Francisco, New York, and Austin and received the same positive feedback.

I sent out the following announcement on our blog later Tuesday morning.

Title: Oracle Buys Involver

Author: Don Beck, CEO

Today we are excited to announce that we have signed an agreement for Oracle's purchase of Involver and we expect the transaction to close in the second half of 2012. The proliferation of social media has changed the way that organizations and consumers interact. Consumers want to have anytime access to information, reviews and recommendations – online and through their mobile devices – from a growing number of social networks. Companies are looking to harness the full potential of social media to increase brand loyalty, connect with potential customers and anticipate buyers' needs. Social savvy customers expect brands to build social campaigns that are engaging, easy to navigate and that provide a consistent experience across multiple touch points.

The combination of Involver with Oracle is expected to create the most advanced and comprehensive cloud-based social solution, across marketing, sales and service touch points. Our technology is expected to extend Oracle's social platform to help customers more easily and cost-effectively collaborate and build engaging applications and social experiences across social networks and the Open Graph.

This acquisition is a combination of the best of both worlds; we will be combining our industry leading social marketing solutions with the comprehensive Oracle Cloud. We are pleased to bring Oracle's experience to our customers who will benefit from access to a suite of social offerings which include: social listening and monitoring capabilities acquired from Collective Intellect, social service capabilities from RightNow and additional publishing and analytics capabilities from Vitrue. Involver customers will also benefit from Oracle's comprehensive support and service through their global scale and reach.

Our management and employees are expecting to join Oracle, bringing domain and social expertise to the Oracle team. We are extremely excited about the prospects of this combination and are continuing to work diligently on bringing innovative technology to market place.

I would like to extend a personal thank you, on behalf of our co-founders, Noah Horton, Rahim Fazal and myself; to the Involverites for your unwavering commitment to providing comprehensive, innovative and creative solutions for the social marketing industry. Your expertise and willingness to always go the extra mile has brought us to this incredible turning point, not only for Involver, but for the world of social technology solutions.

As a team, we are committed to keeping our customers
and followers informed; and will provide updates as
more news becomes available.

For more information on this announcement, please
visit oracle.com/involver.

I wanted all correspondence to include a reference to Rahim and
Noah. They were the face of Involver, not me. They invested more
than five years building the company, not me. The company would
not be here today without their leadership!

In the days immediately after the close, I found myself having
private discussions with many employees who were trying to
determine if joining Oracle would be a good career move. Some
already had offers from other social-media companies based in San
Francisco that offered more base salary and incentive compensation,
as well as potentially lucrative stock option grants. I was very sincere
with my comments and advice. I shared with them that I had nothing
to gain if they stayed with Oracle or joined another company. From
this perspective, I had credibility with some these confused employees
who were looking for career guidance.

I told them that they were extremely talented and that the offers
from outside parties would always be there. I encouraged them not
to be distracted by these offers when evaluating what Oracle could
do for their careers. I felt large-company experience would be very
good for our valued employees, but they had to understand the pros
and cons of what they were getting by joining Oracle.

I stressed the resources, training, experience, and opportunity to
make money at Oracle as being strong reasons to join the company.
I also told them there would be times they would become frustrated
with the decision bureaucracy associated with large companies.
Decisions that could be made by approaching me in the lobby of our
office may take three or four levels of management approval at Oracle.
Large, publicly traded companies required this check-and-balance
system. This was less important in small, privately held start-ups.

I told them to give Oracle at least ninety days and in that time to assess their personal list of pros and cons of working for the company. If at this time they decided to stay at Oracle, then stay at least one year to gain the full experience that a company like Oracle could provide to them both personally and professionally.

I felt this advice was well received.

The Industry Gets More Interesting:

THE CONSOLIDATION OF THE social-media marketing industry that had been predicted by numerous industry analysts had become a reality. But it was not over just yet. By the end of August, Google had announced that it had acquired Wildfire for what was reported to be an approximate $250 million valuation. It was reported at the time of acquisition that Wildfire had grown to 400 employees and served 16,000 customers. The acquisition would enable enhanced social-media experiences such as contests, sweepstakes, and branded games on Google+.

This acquisition was not surprising, but it did put Google in an interesting spot by competing directly with Facebook. Would Facebook deny Wildfire/Google API access? What would then happen to the 16,000 customers of Wildfire who were mostly on the Facebook platform? The industry continued to get more interesting.

After a slow start, Google+ was starting to gain some momentum with more brands placing bets on the social network. Google had reported that three-quarters of the top hundred brands now had Google+ pages. This compared favorably to the brand participation of Facebook (90 percent) and Twitter (80 percent).

It is important to note that Google+ followers, at 1.3 million, still fell significantly short of industry leader Facebook at 10.3 million Facebook fans. A key reason for brands to be on Google+ may be that it might help the brands be displayed more prominently in search results. This would be a key differentiator for Google+ over incumbent Facebook. The competitive landscape for social-media marketing was really heating up with some of the most prominent players in enterprise software going at each other to gain market share in this ever-changing social-media industry.

It was also reported by the trade press that Google had bid on buying Buddy Media but lost out to Salesforce.com. My efforts to generate a bidding war was unsuccessful for Involver but not for my competitors. It paid off to be the top revenue producer in a hot market.

Conclusion

A WEEK BEFORE THE official closing of the acquisition and the change in control was to occur, an article was published in the *Wall Street Journal* regarding the sale of Silicon Valley start-up Digg for a reported $500,000, a mere fraction of the valuation the company was once reported as being worth. From its last round of funding in 2008, the company was valued at more than $164 million by its investors according to Dow Jones VentureSource.

Digg CEO Kevin Rose had raised more than $45 million in venture funding since its inception in 2004 from prominent investors such as Greylock Partners. In many ways, this was the Silicon Valley dream only in reverse. We often read of the incredible success that young entrepreneurs have when they take their vision, start a business in their garage, and then sell the company for many millions of dollars. Again, the press makes it sound so easy.

Digg is a prime example where a hot social-media company (Digg allows consumers the ability to put together news and other Internet content by posting links on the site's home page) that gained great traction and visibility early on in its history as an aggregator of online news and other content. Investors sought to invest in Digg because it was one of the most highly trafficked stops on the Internet.

The exit of this company was a grim reminder that a successful venture is never guaranteed. Could this have happened to Involver? The answer is absolutely yes.

In fact, with the exploding tech job market in San Francisco, it was becoming more and more difficult to hold on to our good employees. The impact of our country's high unemployment rate and challenging economy has not been as severe to Silicon Valley, especially in downtown San Francisco. I am convinced that if we did not have rumors regarding the pending Oracle acquisition in place, many of our employees would have left. Even before the official announcement, I did nothing to stop the rumors. In fact, I did the opposite to keep the team at Involver.

As I mentioned earlier, many employees would come to me for discussion on their personal career matters even before the official announcement. Everyone knew that an acquisition was imminent. So I always asked them what they knew regarding the rumors running rampant within the company. Everyone stated that we were most likely going to be acquired, and it would be Oracle. I then said the same thing to every employee. I made it clear that I would not confirm or deny the rumors. But hypothetically, if they were true, then this is what it would mean to their personal career aspirations. I sold hard on the idea that a few years working for a large company such as an Oracle would be great for their résumés. It was easy for me to sell this to the employees at Involver, because I truly believed it.

Many of the young entrepreneurs at Involver viewed their careers as a sprint and not a marathon. They were concerned about how they would succeed at a large company when their entire career experience was with start-ups. There was much for these talented young executives to gain with some time at a large enterprise software company like Oracle. I stayed at Oracle for two months after the acquisition to help with employee transition. It was important for me to meet with the Involver employee base to ensure they understood that although this would be a major change in their professional lives, it could also be a positive career move as well.

I was keenly aware of the generation gap that existed with the entire company and me, and I knew it would be a challenge to earn their trust. It was important that I did far more listening than talking during my early days at Involver. What was clear to me was that I had a great deal to learn, not only about our product and market but also the mind-set of the employees. What motivates this generation of technology worker? What are their values? What culture do they thrive in?

It was fun to reflect back to when I was their age and working at IBM. I wore a suit every day and a very starched white shirt. My first decision of the day was what tie I wanted to wear with my shirt and very conservative suit. Office desks were the exact same dimension and lined up to accommodate many entry-level workers. Office sizes were modified based on titles and responsibilities. All first-line managers had the same sized office. The same could be said for second-line managers. We had a very strict code of conduct. No alcohol was ever present on IBM premises. If you had a drink during lunch while with a client (only at the client's request), then you were instructed to work from home the rest of the day. The office was for work and was designed accordingly for the task.

Compare and contrast my old work environment at IBM to the new-generation workspace at Involver. Office desk configurations were designed for maximum collaboration with fellow employees. Work attire was basically what you were comfortable wearing. That mostly consisted of designer jeans and T-shirts. The office Ping-Pong table was critical for stress release, so was the large couch where video games could be played on the big-screen television for hours. Employees came and went as needed, which meant that showing up at noon and working until midnight was a regular occurrence with the development team. A refrigerator was in the middle of the office and was kept stocked with many beverages, including beer. I stressed over the liability of employees drinking on company premise but realized none of these perks were exclusive to Involver. I saw this beverage investment at practically every start-up I visited in Silicon Valley. I was still was concerned with Involver employees and their safety, but to their credit, I never saw this become a problem.

I also rarely wore anything but jeans to work. I showed up early and was usually the first to arrive at the company. I was originally concerned that the office was still relatively empty by nine o'clock in the morning, but by staying late to observe the developers and engineers in action, I personally saw how powerful the energy level was late into the evening. You never had to question the commitment of the team. They all worked extremely hard at their jobs but at different hours of the day.

The immediate future of the technology industry is focused on the youthful enthusiasm around new innovative and creative thinking, and I am sure my hiring raised some concerns. I was not young. I did not have a background as a developer or software engineer. I did not know much about the social-media industry. My concerns were justified.

I remember reading a quote from Mark Zuckerberg at a Y Combinator Startup event at Stanford University in 2007 in which he stressed the importance of being young and technical. He said young people are just smarter. He used the example that most chess masters are younger than thirty. He stated that young people just have simpler lives. They may not own a car. They may not have family. His point was simplicity in life allows you to focus on what's important.

I understood exactly what he was saying. The tech world views entrepreneurship as a young person's game. According to recent statistics from California's Employment Development Department, the great majority of IT-related occupations are dominated by the twenty-five to forty-four age group. Software application developers and Web developers skew closer to the twenty-five and thirty-four group and younger.

This also includes bias toward VC investments. Prominent Silicon Valley investors often talk about youth being an advantage in entrepreneurship. They learn their craft at an early age, often programming in high school. Young entrepreneurs can dedicate their lives to building the next-generation Silicon Valley start-up without the complications of a marriage, mortgage, or college education savings accounts. They can invest hours and hours of guilt-free work into their start-ups. The VC community knows this and supports this lifestyle with their funding investments.

In 2011, well-recognized venture capitalist Vinod Khosla, who is the former cofounder of Sun Microsystems, told a conference audience that people older than forty-five basically die in terms of new ideas. He was not alone. Michael Moritz, chairman of Sequoia Capital, one of the most respected venture firms in Silicon Valley, has portrayed himself as an incredibly enthusiastic fan of very talented twenty-something entrepreneurs starting companies. He says they have great passion and that they don't have distractions like families and children and other things to get in the way.

Rahim and Noah had done a great job when Involver was in its prestart-up phase. This was the time when they formulated their idea for a new company, assessed the total addressable market, and built the business plan with clear milestones over the next three years. They also secured seed funding from known angel investors to develop the minimum viable product to prove the concept that was the foundation of Involver. They were also instrumental in validating their business idea with customer references and revenue attainment, which was critical to getting the attention of VC investors. This was done with a successful series C investment round with Bessemer. When I joined Involver, it was during the next phase of the start-up life cycle, which was to scale the business.

The VC community also changed during this time. Investors became wary of overly optimistic business projections from start-up founders and were also no longer enamored by the unrealistic potential of a start-up growing to an initial public offering. According a report published January 2, 2013, by Thomson Reuters and the National Venture Capital Association (NVCA), the industry saw fewer exits from venture-backed firms from 2011, but their value was higher, on average. For the full year, venture-backed IPOs totaled $21.45 billion, doubling from $10.69 billion in 2011. But strip away the $16 billion that social-networking company Facebook raised in May, and the total actually halved.

The number of venture-backed companies that generated an IPO return to their investors has plummeted from a high of 238 in 2000 to only 49 in 2012. This has also led to a shortfall in capital-invested in start-ups. In 2000, companies backed by venture firms generated $27.4 billion, but the money raised from VC-backed IPOs in 2012 represented only $21.5 billion and more than $16 billion of that was attributed to Facebook alone.

The goal is to identify a truly disruptive idea that can change the way we do business or operate as a society. The VCs invest early to secure a significant percentage of the company for as little money as possible—fund and possibly allocate resources to scale the business and increase the value of the company for a future exit.

The lack of success with our funding endeavors was frustrating but understandable. The VC community looked at Involver as an interesting company but was most likely going to be purchased as the social-media industry consolidated. The return for their investment would be very modest at best representing only a twofold or possibly threefold return on their invested capital. Most industries would jump at a chance to make that return in a relatively short duration of time. This is not the VC model and made our company look unattractive in light of the huge successes VCs pursue that could yield with a hundredfold return or even a thousandfold return by investing in the next Google or Facebook at an early stage. These investors obviously did not see a significant upside of potential in our company.

So why was the acquisition of social-media marketing firms so attractive to large enterprise software companies? Building successful social-media technologies is not easy. Large enterprises not only realize the importance of social media but are looking for the end-to-end solution that companies like Oracle are building for their clients. As mentioned earlier, Gartner predicted that by 2017, the average chief marketing officer would spend more on IT than the company's chief information officer. This is the attraction of social-media marketing for companies like Oracle and Salesforce.com, which will be fighting over market share in this area for years to come.

Many large corporations strive to be more entrepreneurial and rejuvenate their daily operations. They seek to be more nimble and respond quicker to market dynamics. They launch entrepreneurship initiatives to accelerate new product innovation critical to establishing a competitive advantage in their respective markets. They sell the fact that they have an "entrepreneur culture" to new prospective employees seeking a change from the traditional large company bureaucracy.

Unfortunately, most large companies are very bad at being entrepreneurial. They typically find this endeavor more difficult than they expected because large companies are at times stuck in the way they always have done business. Change is often viewed more as a threat than a new way to operate and conduct business. Larger companies may have more funding, resources, and assets, but smaller companies have less internal bureaucracy, faster decision cycles, and no shareholders who demand quarterly financial performance.

Today, individuals who act with a sense of urgency and embrace the persona of an entrepreneur within a large company are called intrapreneurs. According to Intrapreneur.com, the definition is listed as "a person within a large organization who takes direct responsibility for turning an idea into a profitable finished product through assertive risk taking and innovation." These employees can be the driving force behind new product development or are the creative thinkers behind new ideas to redesign internal business processes to reduce unnecessary costs. Companies that embrace this spirit reward the risk takers who think differently than the norm. The not-invested-here syndrome is not tolerated. This new entrepreneurial talent can come from the existing employee ranks or from start-up acquisitions where corporate bureaucracy did not exist. The true intrapreneurs typically have very little tolerance for any unproductive use of their time.

At a start-up such as Involver, we had to take calculated risks in order to survive. We had to quickly adapt to swift changes in the marketplace. We did not have layers of bureaucracy that impeded swift decision making. But many large corporations today are too risk-adverse to entrepreneurial behavior that could lead to breakthrough innovations. These companies are not willing to jeopardize or cannibalize existing revenue streams even if competitive solutions threaten their business future. Product failures of large companies can be very public and could impact quarterly earnings or the confidence of a company's shareholders. This thinking is a major inhibitor to the entrepreneurial spirit so important to succeed in today's business world.

This risk-tolerant entrepreneurial spirit must permeate across all business functions and be completely supported by all layers of management. This leadership must recognize the change agents who are making this spirit a reality within a large company. They need to establish an environment that will enable this talent to succeed. Fostering an environment where entrepreneurs can succeed and be recognized for their contributions to the business can lead to exciting business results. This philosophical approach to an entrepreneurial culture could lead to a new innovative product or service, as it enables strategies to achieve new levels of growth or rearchitecting existing core business processes that achieve greater customer satisfaction.

Start-ups are also typically resource constrained. Involver was no different. But this resource constraint was actually critical to our innovation. We could not afford to focus on anything outside our core competency. This relentless focus on our core value was a great enabler of our development team's success.

There is no time to lose focus. This resource-constrained mentality does not often exist in larger corporations. For Involver, our innovation was necessary for our survival. Unlike larger corporations, Involver did not have the financial resources to try multiple things within our development and engineering teams. We had to be creative in everything we did as a company.

Large company acquisitions of start-ups are on the rise, especially in the high-technology sector. It is a fast way to acquire entrepreneurial talent and expertise. I can assure you that Oracle had very little social-media skills in the company before the acquisition of Involver and Virtue. Involver's commitment to the developers who used our platform was a key reason for the Oracle acquisition. This was an influx of skills critical for Oracle's social-media vision.

All too often large corporations hire new employees to fill a spot on an organizations chart, but start-ups, including Involver, hire to fill a process need. Little attention was paid to organizational structure, management span of control, or reporting structure. It was to fill a skill set that could accelerate a core process, such as delivering a product to market faster. Any hiring decision was not trivial in that any new employee had to be able to deliver value immediately. We did not have and couldn't afford a vast onboarding structure. The more executive structure or management layers that exist, the more difficult it is for any company to make decisions.

The acquisitions made by Oracle, Salesforce.com, and Google were not about gaining additional revenues or expansive profits. This was all about gaining valuable technology and skilled resources to address future market needs. These companies just got a lot closer to recognizing the opportunity associated with social CRM. The next step is to incorporate this technology and create a social-media stack that sits on top of their business application solution portfolio. Although it's not an easy task, the first to market reaps the largest benefits.

The experience at Involver made me a far better executive, and I am truly grateful for the lessons learned from this young and talented team. I saw firsthand the entrepreneurial spirit at Involver. I fed off their energy. The young executives at Involver backed their words with actions. I learned the importance of giving our best creative developers the time for product innovation and breakthrough thinking. I encouraged open dialog on new ideas and where Involver needed to invest in our market. I saw the value of a small but diverse workforce where complementary skills meshed for the good of the company.

I was fortunate to have two founders at Involver who had the knowledge and experience to think differently than many of their entrepreneurial peers. I constantly wonder what we could have accomplished if we had received funding. I know this thinking isn't healthy, but I really felt we had something special at Involver. I had great confidence in the founders of Involver and felt they epitomized the entrepreneurial spirit.

What is it about the spirit of an entrepreneur that allows an individual to pursue his or her passion when the odds of failure are so much greater than the probability of success? How can an entrepreneur ride the incredible highs and lows of running a start-up and not become discouraged? To me, Rahim exemplified the entrepreneurial spirit every day at Involver. I saw passion in his daily activities, including a relentless commitment to the success of our company. Regardless of the challenge, he found ways to overcome what seemed at times insurmountable obstacles to our success.

They say that entrepreneurs are not born but are shaped by experiences in their lives. This would explain Rahim's career from starting his own company in high school and eventually selling it for $1.5 million to becoming the founder of Involver.

He also adapted to his environment, including going from being the CEO to reporting to a CEO. It was not easy for him, but he made up his mind to make this personal disappointment into a success for the company. Not many could have embraced this challenge with such professionalism. He understood that this was the decision of the board and that he was going to learn from this experience.

He could have made life difficult for me and other employees by not being supportive of the company's new direction. Rahim did the opposite. He demonstrated great leadership by showing to all employees his commitment to the new direction. He was confident that this learning experience would help him in his future endeavors. I will forever be grateful for his support and remain completely confident that Rahim's greatest career accomplishments are in his future.

We learned a great deal from each other, but we also found out by working so closely together that we had a great deal in common. Our integrity, work ethic, and commitment were completely aligned. We both realized how much we could learn from each other. We both had positive attitudes, regardless of the obstacles we were facing. And maybe most important, we never lost our sense of humor. I know I fed off his optimism, and I hope he did the same with me.

I also learned a great deal from this new generation of technology worker. The Involver employee was extremely talented and highly skilled in his or her job description. They were all passionate about the technology they were building and the benefit society would recognize from their labor. Working hard to achieve financial rewards was a motivation, but also, each employee seemed to want to make our world a better place. This inspired me and gave me a reason to believe in this next generation.

I had my own agenda for joining Involver. To me, it was time to reinvent my professional life. I had success in the enterprise software industry as a senior sales and marketing executive. But after thirty years with this job discipline, my learning curve was on a downward spiral. I was no longer challenged with what I did very well for a living. I was always a calculated risk taker in my career, and I wanted to learn new skills and experiences. Involver gave me both.

My time at Involver was never easy. Long hours and daily frustrations and challenges were the norm. Being a first-time CEO could not have been a better learning experience. Learning a new industry sector such as social media was exhilarating. Learning from the new generation of technology workers, especially two visionary founders, was far more valuable than I could ever have expected. Nothing could have prepared me for the challenges I experienced at Involver, but because I had this unique experience, I truly am a far better executive today.

I also learned a great deal about the next generation of technologist focused on redefining many aspects of the high-tech industry. The future in the technology industry looks bright. This generation thinks differently. They are willing to make many personal and professional sacrifices to achieve success as entrepreneurs.

To say the Involver experience was interesting would be a gross understatement. To say it was challenging would also be a gross understatement.

So let's summarize this wild ride:

- Received a verbal employment offer to join the company only to have me put on hold for months until an unsolicited offer from another company was evaluated.
- Went through another full round of interviews after the unsolicited offer was rejected.
- Met with close to fifty venture capital firms, many multiple times, only to learn that we would not receive required

investments to scale our business. Learning the hard way that if you are fourth in your industry and have not found a way to be disruptive to your competition, then you probably will not get funded.

- Lack of funding led to multiple bridge loans—very expensive bridge loans.
- There was never a day at Involver when cash was not a concern. I never had more than six months of funding.
- An employee payroll deadline causing the founders and me to write personal checks for $60,000 so that payroll could be met. This loan would eventually be repaid when the final bridge loan was secured.
- Learned of the class-action lawsuit against Involver that was later dropped but still caused anxiety with the executive team.
- Received a term sheet from Oracle with only three months of cash remaining. Would we have enough cash to complete the acquisition on time?
- Our best business partner announced two weeks after the Oracle term sheet that it would terminate our agreement and migrate customers off Involver's platform.
- Hired investment banker only to learn during the M&A road show that the company was being acquired.
- Oracle announced the acquisition of Vitrue while due diligence continued on a term sheet with Involver. Again, this caused great stress for the Involver executive team. Was Involver being used as negotiation leverage with Vitrue? Why would Oracle need both companies?
- Salesforce.com bought Buddy Media, causing another distraction within the Involver employee base. Oracle and Saleforce.com had acquired our two main competitors. Without knowing of our term sheet, the Involver employee base were concerned about who else could still be interested in acquiring our company.
- Facebook IPO was a disappointment and impacted valuations and funding of the social media marketing industry.

- Having complied with all required due diligence material in order to sign merger agreement on June 26 (the target date) only to see that come and go due to unfulfilled legal discussions. The delay caused another payroll to occur, completely depleting our cash reserves. This was a major concern with Oracle and was potentially a deal killer.
- In July, immediately after the announcement of Oracle acquiring Involver, Google announced the acquisition of Wildfire for an approximate $250 million.

All of this happened within a span of fourteen months.

At the end of each week, I looked like I had run a marathon with a fifty-pound backpack. It is always nice for my wife to greet me after a long week at Involver by commenting how worn out I looked to her. She often asked if it was worth it. My answer was always yes.

Would I do it again? You bet. I will look back on my experience at Involver with great memories. I look forward to tracking the careers of the young and talented professionals whom I worked with during the past fourteen months. It was truly a wild ride!

I found it ironic that two days after the closing of the transaction, my cell phone service was turned off due to a lack of payment. The life of a start-up CEO is never boring.

Special Thanks:

I HAVE MANY PEOPLE to thank for my experience at Involver.

First and foremost, I must thank my wife and children for allowing me to make the personal sacrifices to achieve this career milestone. I was away from my family a great deal during my time at Involver, and I could not have been as dedicated to the success of the company without their support. My family is a source of my inspiration both in my personal life and professional life.

I also want to thank Byron Deeter. It is clear to me that he submitted my name as a candidate for the CEO opportunity at Involver. This was my first CEO role, and I know now that I had competed for the position with far more experienced candidates. His vote of confidence was greatly appreciated.

I can't imagine a better coach and mentor for a new CEO than Steve Walske. He was an extremely gifted and successful CEO, and I greatly valued his insight and advice during my tenure at Involver. He was always there when I needed him.

The angel investors were also invaluable during my time at Involver and were very instrumental to our successful exit. Preetish Nijhawan and Neeraj Gupta from Cervin Ventures and Alnoor Shivji, a general partner with Global Asset Corporation were extremely supportive and very patient throughout the acquisition process. Alnoor's offer to provide any necessary cash to complete the acquisition right before announcement was critical to our success. I greatly valued this team of investors and their commitment to the success of Involver.

The employees at Involver were very special to me. I became energized by their enthusiasm and commitment to the success of the company. Many stayed with us through some very tough times. Many had competing offers from other firms but stayed with Involver until the end. For that, I will always be grateful.

Finally and most important, I want to thank Involver's two founders, Rahim Fazal and Noah Horton. They too took a risk on a first-time CEO, and their efforts made my experience at Involver extremely rewarding. I say publicly now that I learned more from these two entrepreneurs than they ever learned from me. They were true business partners for me during my tenure at Involver, and I am proud to call them my friends today.

DON BECK JOINED INVOLVER, a social-media marketing company, as chief executive officer in September 2011. The company was sold to Oracle in July 2012. Before Involver, Don held key executive positions in numerous companies, including Webroot, Postini (sold to Google in 2006), Adobe, JD Edwards, and IBM. Beck has more than thirty years of experience in the high-tech industry. He holds a BA in marketing from Michigan State University and an MBA from Miami University. He is an active mentor with Tech Starts in Boulder, Colorado.

His wife, Susan, and their three children reside in Castle Pines Village, Colorado.

CPSIA information can be obtained at www.ICGtesting.com
Printed in the USA
LVOW10s1222040516

486666LV00002B/234/P